TRANSLA
GOD

HEARING GOD'S VOICE FOR YOURSELF
AND THE WORLD AROUND YOU

SHAWN BOLZ

FOREWORD BY BILL JOHNSON

Translating God
Hearing God for Yourself & the World Around You

Copyright © 2015, Shawn Bolz

Special discounts are available on quantity purchases by corporations, associations, and others. Orders by US trade bookstores and wholesalers—for details, contact the author via the website above.

Unless otherwise indicated, all Scripture quotations are taken from THE MESSAGE. Copyright © by Eugene H. Peterson 1993, 1994, 1995, 1996, 2000, 2001, 2002. Used by permission of NavPress. All rights reserved. Represented by Tyndale House Publishers, Inc.

Scripture quotations marked (NIV) are taken from the Holy Bible, New International Version®, NIV®. Copyright © 1973, 1978, 1984, 2011 by Biblica, Inc.™ Used by permission of Zondervan. All rights reserved worldwide. www.zondervan.com The "NIV" and "New International Version" are trademarks registered in the United States Patent and Trademark Office by Biblica, Inc.™

Scriptures marked (CJB) are taken from the Complete Jewish Bible by David H. Stern. Copyright © 1998. All rights reserved. Used by permission of Messianic Jewish Publishers, 6120 Day Long Lane, Clarksville, MD 21029. www.messianicjewish.net.

Scripture quotations taken from the New American Standard Bible®,
Copyright © 1960, 1962, 1963, 1968, 1971, 1972, 1973,
1975, 1977, 1995 by The Lockman Foundation
Used by permission." (www.Lockman.org)

Editor: Sally Hanan, www.inksnatcher.com
Interior Design: Renee Evans, www.reneeevansdesign.com
Cover design: Yvonne Parks, www.pearcreative.ca

First Edition, 2015
ISBN: 978-1-942306-19-1

Publisher: ICreate Productions, 225 South Chevy Chase Drive, Glendale, CA 91205,
www.bolzministries.com

Shawn Bolz's new book, *Translating God*, is an amazing read, full of practical insight and interesting powerful stories that illustrate his teaching points. I read the book in one sitting on a flight to Asia and found it difficult to stop reading. I encourage anyone who wants to learn more about prophecy to buy and read *Translating God*.

I not only want to recommend the book, I want to recommend the author. I remember praying for him about twenty years ago when he did not have a well-known ministry, and I want to let the reader know that Shawn has developed into a very healthy prophetic minister of some very powerful and accurate words that have greatly encouraged many.

RANDY CLARK,
Speaker, Founder Global Awakening
Author and coauthor of over forty books, including There Is More!

One of the goals of my life is to see an honor-based culture come into being in our community of believers, particularly among the prophetic community. We cannot continue in insecurity, competition, and jealousy. I have personally known Shawn Bolz and observed his ministry journey for well over twenty years. The book you hold in your hands is the fruit of the "joining of the generations." With years under his belt, a giftedness that is undeniable, and a lifestyle that exalts Christ Jesus, it is my honor to commend to you the ministry and writings of Shawn Bolz.

JAMES W. GOLL,
Speaker, Founder Encounters Network, Prayer Storm, and God Encounters Training online school, Author of over twenty-five books, including The Lost Art of Intercession *and* The Seer

Although I have read numerous books on prophecy, I can't say that many of them have enthralled me, but this one has! As I went through *Translating God*, I came to admire greatly Shawn Bolz's transparency, humility, and especially ability to analyze different aspects of prophecy. His astute biblical and theological comments provide a solid basis for understanding his message and putting it into practice. I know you will love this book!

C. PETER WAGNER,
Speaker, Vice President Global Spheres, Inc.
Author of over fifty books, including Churchquake! *and* Acts of the Holy Spirit

I've known Shawn Bolz for years now, and I've ministered with him in many situations. I want to wholeheartedly endorse his newest book, *Translating God*. This book will help you as you seek to have open ears to hear and heed the wonderful voice of God. Also, you will grow in your desire to draw ever closer to God. Your life will be greatly enriched and enlightened by devouring this book. It is a delight to be a friend to Shawn, as well as a ministry partner.

BOBBY CONNER,
Speaker, Cofounder Eagles View Ministries
Author of multiple books including the Shepherd's Rod *series*

Shawn Bolz is a prophetic voice to this generation who understands what matters most: our abiding relationship with the Lord. Your life and your ministry will be sharpened and enriched as you answer this holy invitation in *Translating God*: to stay raised and seated with Christ in heavenly places. It is from this position that we can dream with God and love people powerfully.

GEORGIAN BANOV,
DD honoris causa, Cofounder Global Celebration

It's not often that we get to see a prophetic gift mature in front of our own eyes. I am so thankful for Shawn Bolz and his approach to life and the nature of God. Our people here at Bethel Church, Redding, have been deeply impacted over the years by what Shawn carries. Every time he visits our church, we experience promotion and increase. *Translating God* is a must-read for anyone interested in learning how God sees people and how he interacts and engages with us. It will take you to another level.

ERIC JOHNSON,
Sr Pastor Bethel Church, Redding, CA. Author of Momentum *and* Christ in You

Shawn Bolz's book is filled with refreshing and practical encouragement about delivering good news to all people in times of darkness and instability. *Translating God* is an essential message about our ability to impart hope and God's sincere love through prophetic ministry. It is an honor to know Shawn and see the acceleration of grace and maturity in his ministry. Seize the opportunity to "do the stuff" and you'll see that it really works!

MICKEY ROBINSON,
Speaker, Author of Falling into Heaven

I believe that this is the most important book I have ever read on the subject of the prophetic. Shawn has laid out heart priorities that are indispensable for anyone wishing to function or grow in the prophetic. This book invites us to fully step into a New Testament wineskin of attitude, transparency, and accountability that has been notoriously absent in prophetic circles. Shawn's own decades of experience and high level of prophetic gifting give this book a desired credibility factor. I read this book cover to cover and strongly recommend it for anyone desiring to function in or pastor the prophetic.

JOHNNY ENLOW,
Speaker, Founder RISE—a training and equipping center
Author of The Seven Mountain series, among others

Shawn has tapped into something so powerful and exciting, it opens a new door of possibility. I am very keen to see if what Shawn experienced can be activated in others. If so, it is a game changer for the body of Christ. This is the stuff the millennium is likely to produce, and it makes perfect sense that it shows up now, at the end of the church age, in a young man who has tasted the powers of the age to come.

DR. LANCE WALLNAU,
Business Consultant, Director The Lance Learning Group
Author of Invading Babylon *and* Turn the World Upside Down, *among others*

The supreme call and purpose of the prophetic is to release and reveal the love of the Father to a world longing to hear and see. I have witnessed Shawn manifest this reality time and time again while we have traveled the globe together. He carries authority to write this message simply because he lives it.

SEAN FEUCHT,
Musician and Founder Burn 24-7, Coauthor of Fire and Fragrance

I have known and observed the ministry of Shawn Bolz for years. He is a true prophet to our generation with a unique pulse on the redemptive and loving nature of God. He is a gifted communicator and writer, able to not only communicate God's word but God's ways. I am so grateful for who he is and what he brings to the body of Christ.

FAYTENE GRASSESCHI,
Speaker, Artist, Musician, Founder TheCRY Movement and MYCanada
Author of Marked *and* Stand on Guard

In 2001, when I began writing *The School of the Seers*, I spent two years reading every book I could find on the prophetic, angels, discernment, and dreams and visions; over 150 in all. I wish this book from Shawn Bolz had existed then! A huge amount of mistakes and heartache could have been avoided simply by reading the core truths in this book. This is not another book about what certain colors mean or how to interpret spooky dreams. This book speaks to the heart of the prophetic learner and deals with the soil of the heart, because if the soil is good, then the harvest can be good. The stories Shawn shares are memorable and stunning, and the points regarding speaking from the heart of God and being accountable for accuracy rates are so refreshing. This book is a quick read so buy it, read it, and then read it again!

DR. JONATHAN WELTON,
Speaker, Founder The Welton Academy
Author of Normal Christianity, Eyes of Honor, *and* The School of Seers

The world has changed and so must the church. In a world where hope is discouraged, vision is blurred, and people are desperate to know there is a God who loves them, *Translating God* is an essential guide and gift to the church for training, enlightenment, and equipping. Shawn not only trains the church how to "lower the bridge" of communication to the God-hardened, godless, and God-confused; he also breathes God's love back into our hearts by way of encouragement and edification.

As an evangelist to some of the most difficult places in our country and world, it's of major importance for us to have such a resource at our fingertips to help us be more effective there. This book will help us communicate not only the existence of God, but the truth that he desperately loves people. I highly recommend it as a significant tool for today's harvest.

CINDY MCGILL,
Speaker, Founder Hope for the Harvest Ministries
Coauthor of What Your Dreams Are Telling You

Translating God is a book the church has been waiting for. Shawn Bolz carefully walks us through his journey of discovering the God who is not "counting their trespasses against them." This book is a practitioner's manual that encourages and instructs; it's refreshing, biblically balanced, and experientially inspiring. I believe this is a now word for every church that's hungry for a relevant and on-point prophetic ministry.

BISHOP JOSEPH L. GARLINGTON,
Sr., Presiding Bishop Reconciliation!, an International Network of Churches and Ministries
Senior Pastor of Covenant Church of Pittsburgh

What I love most about *Translating God* is how God uses the prophetic to show his facets of love for us. Story after story demonstrates how God's heart is poured out for his children. He will use whatever it takes to love someone into his kingdom. God is jealous for his bride and is after us. Shawn, as a young boy and now as an adult, has stewarded the prophetic in a natural way that has been beautiful to watch. He has done a wonderful job with this book in sharing his revelation on how love should be the main goal of our prophetic gift, especially when serving others.

BENI JOHNSON,
Speaker, Sr Pastor Bethel Church, Redding, CA
Author of The Happy Intercessor, Prayer Changes Things, *and* What If

I love this new book *Translating God* by Shawn Bolz. It's both a practical guide and cutting-edge work that is a must-read for all who are hungry to grow in the art of hearing God. Not only is Shawn a personal friend, but he is one of the premier voices in prophetic ministry today whose gift of revelation and delivery in ministry to individuals is second to none. If you are hungry to grow in the prophetic and move in the gifts of revelation, then the insight and impartation in this book are must-reads for you! I highly recommend this book.

JEFF JANSEN,
Speaker, Founder Global Fire Ministries International
Senior Leader of Global Fire Church and Global Connect. Author of Glory Rising, Furious Sound of Glory, *and* Enthroned

Finally! A book about prophecy that sees love as a higher goal than knowledge, focuses on building relationships more than being accurate, and calls prophets to be accountable for the revelation they receive. I was moved to tears several times reading the prophetic stories in this book because they show how deeply God loves us. Most of all, I felt that I had found a prophet after God's own heart, a prophet who had learned to love (see John 13:34-35 and John 15:12-17). I love this wonderful book.

STACEY CAMPBELL,
Speaker, Cofounder Revival NOW! Ministries and Be a Hero
Coauthor of Praying the Bible *and* Ecstatic Prophecy

Shawn Bolz has one of the most extraordinary and accurate prophetic ministries I know of, which is why I'm excited about this book! Shawn has an ability to take the hyper-mystical out of the prophetic and make it accessible to everyone who is hungry for intimacy with God. Thankfully, that is captured in this authentic book, which emanates grace, truth, and the love of God from every page.

The powerful testimonies and practical teaching in this book will equip you to hear the voice of God and release prophetic insight and encouragement to yourself and others. If you've had experience in prophetic movements, this book is a major heart correction. It marries sound biblical teaching with God's character and nature. Whether you are called to minister behind a pulpit or in the marketplace, this book is for you. Read this book and then put what you learn into practice.

WILL FORD,
Director, Marketplace Leadership, Christ for the Nations Institute
Author of Created for Influence: Transforming Culture from Where You Are

I've always been on the hunt for prophetic books that capture the heart culture of the prophetic by a person who is living proof of what the Father has in mind for this precious gift. My great friend Shawn Bolz embodies all of the above.

This book has inspired me and imparted to me. I truly believe that Shawn is a prototype prophet for an emerging breed of prophetic vessels that will release the third great awakening and reformation in the house. His paradigm of love for humanity and intimacy with the Father is truly what this new breed must carry. I'm convinced that this book will be a classic training tool used to release a culture and the DNA of Jesus-style prophets. It will help many become attuned to the wavelength of heaven.

SEAN SMITH,
Speaker, Founder Sean Smith Ministries and Pointblank International
Author of Prophetic Evangelism *and* I Am Your Sign

Translating God reminds me of Bill Hammond's book *Prophets and Personal Prophecy* as far as how heavy and important the content is. Hammond's book was a huge language giver, protocol setter, and inspiration to many. What that book was for its time (and still is for our time today) is exactly what this book is for this time and this generation (and those to come). What God has entrusted Shawn with is rare, but it must become widespread!

God was very intentional when he connected 1 Corinthians 13 (the love chapter) and 1 Corinthians 14 (the gifts chapter), because God's great power and love are dynamically connected to one another. You cannot have one without the other. *Translating God* is an amazing testimony of this reality. Not only was I encouraged by reading it, but I have seen and experienced firsthand both the great love and gift (power) that Shawn flows in. Every generation has been given the chance to change the world, and I truly believe that Shawn and this important book will do just that.

RICK PINO,
Musician, Founder Heart of David Worship and Missions Center

MEMORIAL

In memory of Bob Jones, whose childlike faith in the supernatural helped me believe in my own experiences. Your encouragement and trust and the hours and hours you spent with me, showing me that God in me was as powerful as God in you, will never be forgotten. I still don't understand half of the prophetic words you gave me, but the other half developed what I am doing now. I know that now that you are in heaven, your conversation with God has only increased, and we are all benefiting from your eternal state. I am so glad that this project, and many others like it (by all your spiritual family here on earth), is making your eternal treasury full. Our fruit is your fruit!

DISCLAIMER

I love the prophetic so much, but it is mostly a personal ministry between God and an individual or group. Therefore I changed most of the names of people in the book, or I made the stories purposely more vague than I wanted to.

While I love the glory they carry, I want to honor the privacy of the presidents, billionaires, celebrities, and church leaders that I told stories about, even if they were okay with me telling who they were at times.

CONTENTS

FOREWORD

one   A SIMPLE GOAL OF LOVE

two   THE REVELATION OF REVELATION

three   WHY I EAGERLY DESIRE THE PROPHETIC

four   THE PROPHETIC IS FIRST A CULTURE OF OUR HEARTS

five   THE NATURE OF NEW TESTAMENT REVELATION

six   REVELATION, A STEP PAST DISCERNMENT

seven   THE WAY GOD COMMUNICATES

eight   THE REVELATION GIFTS

nine   PROPHETIC POWER IS RELATIONAL POWER

ten   REVELATION—EVERYONE GETS TO PARTICIPATE

eleven   ACCOUNTABILITY, A NEW WAY TO GROW

twelve   RESPONSIBILITY IN REVELATION

thirteen   PUTTING IT INTO PRACTICE

ABOUT THE AUTHOR

ACKNOWLEDGMENTS

FOREWORD
by Bill Johnson

I am amazed by Shawn Bolz's book *Translating God: Hearing God's Voice for Yourself and the World Around You*. It is one of the most encouraging books I've ever read. As such, it is filled with great biblical insight and is saturated with God stories—the kind that give hope and draw the reader near to a wonderfully perfect Father. I am moved, deeply moved. At times, even to tears.

Shawn has been a dear friend for many years. I have watched with wonder as God has used him to display his perfect love for people through words of knowledge and prophecy. I find the wisdom with which Shawn stewards this gift to be very inspiring. His transparency in the prophetic process makes the rest of us believe God could use us in a similar fashion. One of the statements found in this book helps us understand why: "This is the goal of prophecy: to connect people to the empowering nature of God so they can become like him and display his marvelous nature to all the earth." The prophetic connects people to the nature of God so they will become like him and reveal him. Brilliant!

The prophetic is such a wonderful part of our life in Christ. I can't imagine what my life would have been like for the last forty years without the prophets; they have made me richer in every possible way. Perhaps that's why the enemy of our souls likes to distort their ministries so much. Here, too, Shawn adds a depth of wisdom that should calm the hearts of those who have only experienced heartache and disappointment through this ministry. The time for the authentic has come.

I've been amazed to watch how God sets people up to receive his love through precise words of knowledge. Shawn's gift in this area has become a sign and a wonder on a whole new level in recent times. Witnessing Shawn's increase in precision has released several in our ministry to take greater risks to see if God would use them similarly. And, in fact, he does. The results are quite remarkable. Why are so many growing in this vital expression of God's heart? I credit Shawn's practical approach to hearing from God, along with his wisdom in stewarding his gift, while maintaining love as the centerpiece of the prophetic ministry.

As much as I love healing and all the other manifestations of God's love, I've never seen anything cut to the heart of a person quicker than an accurate prophetic word. In a recent study, several thousand people were asked what one question they would ask God if they could be assured he would answer. The number one question, asked more times than number two and three combined, was: "What is my purpose in life?" Perhaps this is why the prophetic is so powerful. When it's done well, people realize they are known and loved by God, who then leads them to their purposes. This process is one of the most glorious things I've ever witnessed. This is where my eyes are regularly filled with tears. God really is love, and that is seen through his passion for people coming into their reason for being. *Translating God* is filled with such stories, but the stories do more than encourage, although that would be enough for me. The stories are so inviting that they automatically instill courage so that the reader might grow in these kinds of Holy Spirit expressions too. That makes books like this *priceless!* In my heart, I can see countless people growing in their ability to manifest God's love in a way that has an immediate impact on people's lives, simply by reading this book.

Read, enjoy, and be changed. The world is crying out for God to manifest himself through his gifts flowing through his people.

BILL JOHNSON
Senior Pastor, Bethel Church, Redding, CA
Author of *When Heaven Invades Earth* and *Hosting the Presence,* among others

CHAPTER 1

A SIMPLE GOAL OF LOVE

I was sitting next to a man on a plane ride to Australia, so I struck up a conversation with him and found him to be very engaging, even though he seemed a little distracted. We talked about life and family and careers. He was working for oil companies, and this was his last month traveling the globe for them. He was particularly fascinated by our work against human trafficking and had not heard of the current research or grass roots efforts by groups like ours. He appeared very touched.

At one point he got up and went to the bathroom, and that's when I heard the voice of the Holy Spirit: *He hasn't told you the whole truth. He is not working for oil companies but is the air marshal. I want to encourage him about his retirement, which is coming fast.* I also heard a word of knowledge and got his wife's name; the place he always wanted to visit in Europe in his retirement; and knowledge about his daughter, who was pregnant with complications. I was so overwhelmed that when he got back, I didn't know what to say.

He initiated though, not knowing what he was inviting, and started right in about God. "You were talking about your relationship with God and how you felt called to what you were doing. How did you know you were called?"

I loved the lead into my word for him. I began to explain how real Jesus is and how he has so much love for us and is present in our lives. Then I asked him if I could share with him some things I felt God was showing me in order to encourage him. He was very excited and said yes.

"He told me you are the air marshal and that your wife's name is Patricia. He also told me that he wants what you want more than you ever wanted it—like going to the Italian vineyards in southern Italy when you retire. He also told me about your daughter, Anna, and how she is pregnant but experiencing difficulties, and how you prayed and asked him to help her. You told him you would do anything if he would just help her. He wants to help her more than you do, and she and her baby are going to be okay."

He had tears in his eyes the whole time, and when I talked about his daughter, tears streamed down his face. He was gripping both seat handles intensely. "I am not the air marshal!" he said.

I laughed, because he had just received a direct communication from God that impacted him deeply and he was trying to cover his base about his job. "Well, is anything else true of what I felt from God?"

"Yes, all of it!" he said, "but I am not an air marshal." He was covering again.

I just laughed because I knew he was, but thought maybe he was required to say this. We prayed together and exchanged information, and when the rest of the passengers got off of the plane, he stayed behind. I didn't get to say goodbye, because he went up into the cockpit.

When I was at baggage claim I felt a hand on my shoulder. I turned around and it was my new friend.

"I can't believe God showed you I was an air marshal! I had to go and do a background check on you before I talked to you! That was amazing that God showed you all of that! I want to hear from God like that! I feel like everything is right again in my world."

What a statement! I knew he had never felt more loved and connected to God than at that moment, and I knew both of us would never be the same.

The prophetic is one of the greatest tools of love we have. Picture how technology has created a platform of connection in one generation. We can communicate virtually anywhere in the world through smart devices, Internet services, streaming, virtual reality, etc. Technology has created the connection for anyone to talk anywhere to any of his friends, and to even make new ones. You can become part of an online community that you would have never had access to without it.

The prophetic is meant to be like this; it is the technology or smart device to our spiritual love. It is the tool that accelerates relationship and creates connection with people, cities, countries, industries, and the world. Through it we see a very real glimpse of God's heart and get to treat people exactly the way God intended them to be treated from the beginning.

As with technology, revelation was not just meant to inspire prophetic gifts, but to help us live with a connection to how God feels and what he thinks. It is supposed to be our way of life—to see people the way God always longed for them to be seen and, from that revelation, to treat them out of his culture of love so that they will want to be the version of themselves we see. (More on that later.)

Having a deep relationship with God that includes authentic friendship will definitely lead you into sharing that kind of relationship and friendship with others. Many people pursuing prophetic gifts are about as close with God as they are with their yearbook friends, but they still insist on trying to *use* prophecy on others. Then they get discouraged about the lack of relational depth developed through the experience. It's because prophetic ministry is about your being a gateway to God's thoughts, emotions, and heart for others *through your connection to him.*

The world is full of 7+ billion pieces of God's heart, and as you get to know him, you begin to absorb his affection for humanity. Your relationship with him is the primary source and goal of revelation.

Throughout this book, I am going to focus on why we should highlight love rather than information as the goal of prophetic ministry. I will bring insight into why God speaks, how he speaks, and how to steward and develop a track record of revelation. I will also challenge other philosophies of how to move in the prophetic that might violate this principle of love. Lastly, you will find pieces of my own journey here so that you can learn from my strengths and failures. I want you to take huge risks, but to do that you might need my examples of how I survived some very real misses.

There is nothing like being a translator who brings good news—news that not only is "feel good" but can transform. I love seeing people connect with God, family, friends, their life purposes, and even just nature because of a useful prophetic word. It's like the puzzle pieces come together in love for them.

On a negative side, though, I have been around so many types of prophetic ministries that I could tell you thousands of stories that would make you laugh, cry, and wonder at what people were trying to accomplish while prophesying. We will definitely get to some of these, but the prophetic gets a bad rap because of the types of personalities that get involved. If God really was responsible for every word that people were claiming were his, then the God of insurance companies truly would exist (with their "acts of God").

I digress. Let's get into this exciting subject and hopefully, even for the experts, I will offer a new twist on a developing subject in the church.

MY NANNY

Before our nanny, Tammy, started working for us, she was one of the leaders in our school of ministry (at our church in Los Angeles). I didn't know her very well, but she and her husband have great friendship chemistry, so I always felt a connection. I taught at the school one evening and I said in front of her class, "I have a list of names for you, Tammy. It's crazy . . . just a bunch of names. Tell me if they make sense." I named all of her children, their spouses, and her grandchildren. At the end I even said, "One more," and discovered her daughter was currently pregnant. Then I told her, "You have given up your family to move out here because God told you to. He will take care of them and bless them while you are blessing his family. He loves them more than you do."

Tammy was hit with solid assurance. She and her husband had made the move from Minnesota to Los Angeles based on a faith journey, and she was relying on faith that it would work out here. She told me later that her only major stress in life was not being with her kids and grandkids, and that it had been very hard for a while. She couldn't believe that God knew their names through me, and it helped her heart know even more that he loved them in a way that even she can't. (Shortly after this she became our nanny, and it's been an amazing experience having her.)

I have been haunted by God saying through me and to me, "I love what you love more than you love it." You know what? Prophecy *proves* this.

A SIMPLE GOAL

The goal of revelation is so simple: See what God sees, hear what God hears, and speak what God speaks so we can all love the way God loves. Revelation is given to us so we can carry a piece of God's heart from eternity into the world.

"We prophecy each time we make known his passionate heart." MIKE BICKLE

JESUS'S LOVE WAS COUNTERCULTURE IN HIS DAY

Jesus was so unconventional. He chose fishermen, tax collectors, and prostitutes, and he used them to reshape the world. Somehow he saw them through different eyes; they looked completely different to him than they did to the world around them. The level of value he treated them with was so uncommon, and *he believed in them*. God even said to Samuel, "You look at the outward appearance. I don't make judgments like that" (see 1 Samuel 16:7), meaning he used a different scale to judge who was worth his investment. So where did this weighing or vision for them come from?

Jesus wasn't just a football coach who saw some people's potential and was trying to upgrade them with his coaching ability. He saw them through a developed lens of love—the Father's point of view. He saw them as though they were restored to their original design, God's original intention, as though they had already fully said yes to his invitation of walking with him, even though they were not yet capable. He didn't treat them as he hoped they would one day be, he treated them as if they were already restored.

Jesus treated people with a worthiness they didn't deserve—an unusual honor bestowed on man. Once you really begin to understand the Gospels, you will understand how much Jesus relied on his friendship with heaven and his Father's revelation of love about each person.

There was a metaphor throughout the Old Testament about the world's eyes and ears being closed to see truth, and this was obviously the state of the union in Jesus's day, yet he treated people as though they could see and hear the hidden or full meaning of what he was doing. It was so counterintuitive to how the Israelites and others were treated that they were personally intrigued. Others who watched Jesus make an investment into folk who didn't seem special were also fascinated. Everybody loves to be "in" on a secret or to be "in the know." Jesus made them feel like they knew the secrets of heaven, and when they looked at him, they somehow did.

When Jesus was moved by compassion, it was not just a feeling he had, but an understanding and conviction of what those people meant to the Father. Their value in the eternal realm was not just based on their immediate healing; Jesus could see what would happen if they had a connection again to God, if they could walk in the fullness of the purposes they were created for. He also saw them as though they were already eternal, and he pulled them into that place just by loving them. Ultimately, he laid down his life to reconnect them to the Father because he believed in the value of that connection.

If we applied this version of revelatory insight to our modern prophetic ministry, it would dramatically change the way we treated each other. So much of prophetic ministry today has lost its higher focus and reduced itself to the mere development of gifts. The real purpose of prophecy is to tie you to your eternal calling to be *in* Jesus—in the best form of yourself that you were designed to be. Prophecies to individuals, cities, ministries, or industries are all supposed to help you catch a glimpse of the *you* that is truly *you*. It is supposed to allow you the feeling of what it is like to be both eternal and spiritual alongside feeling normal and human. It is also supposed to help set your hope on your eternal purpose—to know God the way he has always dreamed of being known by his creation.

Have you ever felt that? It's like what kids feel when they pretend to be superheroes; it's what our emotions experience when watching a movie whose characters overcome their weaknesses and turn into champions; it's that feeling that God is not only awesome, but he wants us to be awesome too. It's empowerment in fullness. It's about life and living life in true fullness (see John 10:10).

I was visiting my friends in the family homeless shelter they used to run in Atlanta, Georgia, and the director, Rose, and I were in a conversation. She was telling me about a man who had left his wife and kids to go hit some street drugs, and how she was so angry at him because she was really believing for their restoration. She wasn't angry in rage; she was angry in belief for him. I watched Rose, who is a normal woman, who in any other occupation should be afraid of street crack addicts, somehow get filled with emboldened courage.

We went into the family side of the shelter and she walked right up to the man who had just come back late from a drug trip. She put her finger in his face and said, "What are you doing? We all believe in you! You have no right to leave your family!" and she just told him his true story again—the love story of his family and of his God. The man kept apologizing to Rose. He could see God in her compassion and her vision for him; to him she was not just a concerned humanitarian, but someone who saw his true value. She brought him back to conviction to turn to what was good, not to what was temporary. He felt in her love for him the possibility of a different life, a better life, and it's those moments that enable us to make some of our best decisions.

When we are loved like that, we feel like a version of ourselves that transcends the limitations of whatever path we have chosen or of whatever hasn't happened for us yet.

It is hard to see prophecy as a love gift when so many recognized prophets (in many denominations and movements) spend their time discerning what we have failed in, what has separated us, or what makes us unworthy. Then they give correction or directive words that don't really help where we are at. Or worse, they pronounce judgment on us because their theology is so tied to performance or what's right and wrong. This can often violate love.

Throughout this book, we are going to define the difference between the common discernment of spiritual information, which is readily available to the whole world, versus actual communication and relationship building with God. His eternal plan is for us to see what he sees, which enables us to love like he loves.

CHAPTER 2

THE REVELATION OF REVELATION

I am a creative person who loves storytelling. Whether through my time as the story director of a video game, a writer of unpublished novels, a film producer, or a motivational speaker to millions of people, I always go through the process of developing a story. I love the power of story. When you understand the story of an individual or a group of people, you can more fully relate to them.

To really understand how prophecy works, the story of John the Beloved is the clearest way to understand the role of the prophetic in the New Testament. John knew he was Jesus's favorite, not because he was the only one highly favored, but because of the quality of love he experienced with Jesus. He called himself the best friend of Jesus, the one Jesus loved. And yet even the amazing friendship they nurtured did not hold the full measure of what John desired until he had his encounter. We can view it through his eyes, because he showed us what he saw through the book of Revelation.

First of all, as someone believing for the prophetic gift, you need to read the book of Revelation in its context (outside of an eschatology book). You need to see the friendship dynamic between John and Jesus. You need to understand John first in order to fully grasp what God revealed to him. Before you care about pretribulation, post tribulation, preterism, or even millennialism, you need to see the dynamic between the man who received the revelation and his God.

John, who claimed to be the best friend of Jesus, was brought to heaven to see something. He was brought to see the key revelation to all other revelations in history. That revelation wasn't just that Jesus was coming back, or that he was a glorious God, or that he had prepared a place for us. The revelation was about *us*.

JOHN, THE FIRST TO SEE JESUS IN HIS FULL GLORY—AN ANSWER TO JESUS'S PRAYER (SEE JOHN 17)

John felt so close to Jesus, and he had one of the deepest relationships with God of anyone in history. His revelation counterbalanced that of the Jews because he represented the love filter; he saw love as a primary goal. John longed to be with Jesus where he was. Revelation 1:

John, with you all the way in the trial and the Kingdom and the passion of patience in Jesus, was on the island called Patmos because of God's Word, the witness of Jesus. It was Sunday and I was in the Spirit, praying. I heard a loud voice behind me, trumpet-clear and piercing: "Write what you see into a book. Send it to the seven churches: to Ephesus, Smyrna, Pergamum, Thyatira, Sardis, Philadelphia, Laodicea." I turned and saw the voice.

I saw a gold menorah with seven branches, And in the center, the Son of Man, in a robe and gold breastplate, hair a blizzard of white, Eyes pouring fire-blaze, both feet furnace-fired bronze, His voice a cataract, right hand holding the Seven Stars, His mouth a sharp-biting sword, his face a perigee sun.

I saw this and fainted dead at his feet. His right hand pulled me upright, his voice reassured me:

"Don't fear: I am First, I am Last, I'm Alive. I died, but I came to life, and my life is now forever. See these keys in my hand? They open and lock Death's doors, they open and lock Hell's gates" (Revelation 1:9-17).

In Revelation 1, the first thing Jesus revealed to John was the fullness of his God nature. The Father brought John to heaven so that John could see Jesus in his true form. John had only seen the human Jesus and the resurrected Son of Man, but never had he seen the fully glorified One. He had never seen his friend the way Jesus truly was. Stop right here and picture that for real. What is that like, to know we can see God the way he truly is? Throws that old superstitious theology of not being able to "see the face of Jesus and live" right out the window, doesn't it? John was just a man and yet he saw. He saw Jesus for who he truly is. This was the first full answer to Jesus's prayer to the Father: "Father, I desire them to be with me where I am. . ." (see John 17:24).

John was so overwhelmed, he fell as though he were dead. This is a part that you and I need to ponder together. Think about that reaction. What did the man who felt so close to Jesus go through *on the inside* when he saw Jesus this way? What caused him to collapse to the point where Jesus had to extend his hand for John to even be able to stand?

After John saw him this way, Jesus spoke about the church he had commissioned the disciples to build—not a specific church, but churches of cities—living organisms of God's nature surrounding relationships, not just structures.

Jesus spoke to John, just as he always had, in dark sayings and parables that weren't just for the church of his day, but that would last until he returned. He wanted all believers to read and interpret them in *their* time. Revelation 2-3 is a must-read for anyone developing a prophetic gift. Read and reread and reread it again, because it says so much in such a short amount of space. Study how Jesus related to John. Read about the revelation Jesus wanted to give the church to sustain it and speak into hearts. It's amazing.

For most people who hear God, having an experience like John's would have been their most monumental encounter ever. Jesus spoke to John about the church, he revealed himself, he told John to write the book of Revelation, and there was enough there to glory in for many lifetimes. The end. But then something unexpected and amazing happened. . . There was more, and what was revealed would change everything!

REVELATION 4—COME UP HIGHER

Yes, modern charismatic conferences and churches have made many cliché terms out of great Scriptures, and this is one of them. But reset your pallet for a minute and listen to a fresh take on this. Get over the familiarity to the Scriptures you have read so many times and let's start anew.

John heard a voice from somewhere in heaven beckoning him even higher into revelation. It was calling him beyond what he could previously see or comprehend. From Revelation 4:19 on, John went on a very incredible journey of seeing all the things that needed to take place before Jesus returned. He saw wars, demons, dragons, harlots, sicknesses, plagues, justice, martyrs . . . so much symbolism! But then, in the midst of such intense revelations, he was brought to the very key point of the book of Revelation: he was to write down every revelation so future generations could understand the heart of God. It would give them the endurance and perspective to overcome anything that came their way. It would be the REVELATION of Revelations.

He came in the heavenly encounter (see Revelation 19) to a space where the multitudes were worshipping and lifting up loud songs, and he understood why as soon as he heard what they were singing about.

"From the Throne came a shout, a command: Praise our God, all you his servants, All you who fear him, small and great! Then I heard the sound of massed choirs, the sound of a mighty cataract, the sound of strong thunder: Hallelujah!

The Master reigns, our God, the Sovereign-Strong! Let us celebrate, let us rejoice, let us give him the glory!

The Marriage of the Lamb has come; his Wife has made herself ready.

She was given a bridal gown of bright and shining linen. The linen is the righteousness of the saints" (Revelation 19:5-8).

John always knew he was the best friend of Jesus, but all of a sudden he was seeing the very desire of the heart of the Father for his Son, the very thing that fueled Jesus's desire to go to the cross: the bride of Christ.

The most amazing thing about what he saw is that she was fully ready. He wasn't just seeing a symbol of a people on the earth *at the time* who were ready for Jesus, but of the *culmination of all* those who loved Jesus and *will* love Jesus *in every generation*. And even more awesome: John was seeing her in absolute perfection, *fully* ready for the wedding day, *fully* prepared, and dressed to marry Jesus.

I remember being in my best friend, Jona's, wedding. I was his best man, and as we stood together waiting for his bride to come around the outdoor curtains, I watched Jona. I don't think I had ever seen anticipation like that on a man before, but maybe it was because I had never felt so connected to anyone who was experiencing it.

The song started and we looked with hope, excitement, love, and rest as she came around the corner. Jona gasped. No really, he literally gasped. I was about to laugh, but stopped when I looked at his face. It said: "God, you are giving me everything I ever desired. She is so beautiful, so worthy of love, so perfect. Thank you!" as tears streamed down his face.

I could feel his joy and praise, and I "knew" it was similar to what John saw in Revelation 19. I felt like John at my friend's wedding. He saw the most perfect form of the bride the Father had helped prepare for his Son. No wonder God could send his only Son into the world to pay such a price—he knew what Jesus was going to get in return, and you know what? We are a beautiful bride! You are totally worth it.

I see you in Revelation 19 and you are amazing! And that's how John saw the church from that point on. He didn't see it as though it might be glorious one day, but as one already established and promised.

SEEING PEOPLE AT THE END OF THE RACE WITH THE TROPHY IN HAND

Now understand, John was dealing with constant church and state politics. He was fighting against a cult that was watering down the truth and fighting for the revelation of how Jesus was to be understood in his generation.

Reality check: He hadn't yet seen a fully prepared people on the earth. He was probably seeing the lack of what wasn't in them or present on the earth. He was fighting for people to receive the basic gospel message of love and the power of the resurrection of

Jesus. When you read his earlier books (John 1, 2, and 3), you get a picture of what he was dealing with. But when he had the revelation of Revelation, when he saw the very object of the desire of God fully prepared for Jesus, he was completely overwhelmed. He was seeing eternity now—the bride made ready to not just serve, but to partner as a creator, to partner as a counterpart, to partner as a daughter/son, to partner as a friend.

I want to interpret or paraphrase Revelation 19:9-10. Here's how I imagine it played out:

REVELATION 19:9-10 PARAPHRASED FOR YOUR UNDERSTANDING

Then the angel looked at John, who had been chosen like a best man in a wedding, and said, "Write to every generation: Blessed are those who are invited to the wedding feast to see this glorious bride and bridegroom married! These are the true words and witness of God. What you are seeing now is the culmination of the story of God! It is the happy ending that will happen and everyone will see it!"

Then John fell at the angel's feet, completely overwhelmed by the beauty of what the Father had prepared for Jesus: the bride of Christ. He just couldn't bring himself to write about her; she was too magnificent, too beautiful. The Father's desire made manifest in all believers throughout all time joined together saying "I DO" to Jesus was just too much for John. It was a thing of utter awesomeness.

"You do it," he said to the angel who told him to write it. "You have seen the same thing and you are an angel, and you're holier than me! I am just a man."

But the angel said to John, "Don't try and give me this responsibility and treat me like I am holier than you or more worthy. I am just a servant—like you and everyone else who understands that mankind was created to be the counterpart of Jesus. This is the very thing the Father has stated since the beginning. This is the testimony we hold. Focus your worship and feelings of holiness or worthiness on God, because what you see here with the bride is God's story unfolded before you. This is what the spirit of prophecy is talking about—the bride made ready for the bridegroom. This is what the spirit of revelation is.

This is probably a fresh way for many of you to see these Scriptures, but it's essential that we understand that when Revelation 19:10 is quoted, it has a subject, and the subject is not just a gift of prophecy. It is a bride who has made herself ready.

This is the goal of prophecy: to connect people to the empowering nature of God so they can become like him and display his marvelous nature to all the earth. I love how in Revelation 19:8 the bride was wearing fine linen, which represented that she had already clothed herself in the nature of Christ and was acting out his standards, values, life choices, and attitude on the earth.

When John came back from this experience, I am sure it changed the way he saw everyone and everything. He could probably no longer see with any value the weakness of individuals or the politics in the church. He was now seeing everyone with a full invitation to be that bride.

AT THE END OF THE RACE WITH TROPHY IN HAND

"It takes no anointing to see what is wrong in people's lives. Tell them something they don't know! See the gold and tell them that." PHIL ELSTON

Paul talked about sports and running races quite a few times. It's such a great picture of the Christian journey. It is also essential to have this in your perspective when you think about prophecy, because it will help set the goal higher for you. Paul talked about every believer needing to run as though he were going to get the prize, because a runner doesn't run the race to get the silver or bronze. He runs for the gold.

When John came back from heaven, he saw the church in a new way. It's like he saw everyone who was running the race already at the end with their first-place trophy or gold medal. In the natural they probably all looked much like the disciples, prostitutes, fishermen, low cast in society, and rich partiers of his day; but in his spirit, John had new eyes of revelation. He could see people as though they were fully ready to say yes on their wedding day. This is how he began to treat everyone.

Talk about fathering and coaching coming from the ultimate place! What would happen if people had treated you, from the time you were a small child, as if you were going to be one of the most important people in history and eternity? What would happen if we chose to treat each other according to our eternal identity now? One of the last great moves of God is going to be the awakening of the whole earth. We'll walk into a functioning place of revelation that empowers people to fully say yes to God and to take on his nature so they can be amazing now, not just in eternity.

REVELATION EMPOWERS YOU TO SEE EVERYONE AROUND YOU AS WINNERS, AS WORTHY

"The glory of God is coming, and it is going to be in his glorious love!" BOB JONES

Your goal in giving revelation to others should be to encourage them that they aren't just good runners in a race, but that they are worthy of the first place prize. Revelation empowers you to see everyone around you as winners, as the bride. It also helps you see how to help people and groups overcome obstacles that would keep them from empowerment.

Much of what the prophetic has been in the past decades has not lined up with the truth of love. It has come from many theologies and self-interested building movements, or even just rigid theology that isn't focused on the big picture of love. You can avoid these traps by not only trying to see each person you bring revelation to as lovable, but by asking God for his eyes to see each one in eternity. God always sees the end before the beginning, and he wants you to too!

"I see you in the future, and you look much better than you look right now." KIM CLEMENT

This is part of the main subject, in every Bible story, of God's endearing love. It is the story of why we prophesy. In other words, prophecy is a tool to see a full picture of those God loves.

CHAPTER 3

WHY I EAGERLY DESIRE THE PROPHETIC

I was just old enough to know that the woman sitting in front of my parents was in pain, and my parents told me it was in her back. They were doing a personal ministry time while at a retreat in the mountains of California. I was only six, and I happened to be propped up on my mom's lap. They prayed for her for quite a while for her back pain to be healed, which was quite a common scenario for me to see at this age because my parents were hungry for God's love to move through healing and the supernatural gifts.

What wasn't common was when my mom felt me fidgeting. Instead of getting irritated with me, she asked, "Is God showing you anything, honey?" To me! A little kid!

I actually did feel like I had heard something. "Is your back hurting because of a car accident?" I asked.

"Yes!" She was shocked that I was participating and getting a word of knowledge.

"God wants to make your back the way it used to be before the accident," I said. Then I got off my mom's lap and laid both my hands on her and prayed, joined by my parents. Together, we watched this woman get completely restored.

Mom and Dad had always been good at including us in their ministry times, but after that it just became their norm to ask if God was showing me anything. It caused me to want to ask God about his heart and desire for people. I was aware of this supernatural kingdom of God that could make people whole again, that could encourage people in the deepest ways, and could help connect them to who they really were, all at the age of six. This formed my view of relationships and of what is possible in my lifetime, and of who God is as a Father.

I love what God's voice does inside of us. It is so forming, so connecting, so relating. There is the original version of us that God the Father intended, and his voice helps to reestablish the feeling of true self or original self.

WERE YOU BORN A SOVEREIGN VESSEL? I DIDN'T HAVE A STAR APPEAR IN THE SKY ABOVE ME, AND YOU PROBABLY DIDN'T EITHER, BUT YOU ARE ENOUGH!

I always knew I was special, but I also felt everyone else was too. My parents taught us that everyone was equal, and they modeled compassion for the poor and the support of women in powerful leadership roles. They valued other races and people groups without prejudice. They weren't perfect, even in these areas, because they hadn't grown up with a mature picture of what that looked like in society or in the church, but I grew up pretty balanced with no segregation perspectives.

When I got around people who were perceived as better because of talent, gifts, authority, titles, positions, etc., I just couldn't relate to it and looked at it as elitism. I actually would want to fight for the underdog to become more empowered. As I got around the prophetic community, most had stories that qualified them to be in the ministry while I'd just had a normal life with parents who raised me to believe God spoke to all Christians. I felt weird because they had fantastic supernatural visitations and I was just normal. How I longed to have their stories . . . before I fell in love with my own. Little did I know it, but this lack of sovereign commissioning into a crazy ministry would help me empower all you other "normal" Christians down the road.

We're used to hearing the spectacular stories told over and over—stories from God's people (called to lead in this generation) having radical conversions from the craziest sinful lives or having special circumstances around their births. These stories have caused a lot of those who have listened to feel separate, not as special, and not anointed at birth. Let me assure you, though, that when we see one who is born this way, it's supposed to remind us all of God's special love for each one of us. We were all made entirely unique and wonderful, with a potential to be one of God's best expressions of himself here on earth. We don't need to have a birthmark prophetically positioned in a sign on our third rib to tell us what the Bible has already told us: We are intricately, beautifully, and wonderfully made.

LONGING FOR SIGNIFICANCE

When I was a teen, I remember asking the big questions: Who am I? What am I? Where should I go to thrive? Is there justice for all the hardship in this world that I am seeing? Can I be significant to God? I began to really pray and try and find out why this amazing God chose me to come onto this earth in this time. Although my family has always been amazing, I couldn't find the tools to define some of these questions. There was a time when I would read the Bible every night and finish it sometimes once a month. I read the New Testament in three-night increments over and over. I was trying to find out if my answers to my questioning heart were in there.

One night, after a long, hard time of pressing in without seeing a lot of fruit, I had a God encounter. I won't describe the entire surroundings of it, but it was while in my parents' house at the age of fifteen. I heard God say, "Go to the family seminar tomorrow." My parents had told my sister and my about a family seminar at a church in Sacramento, and though they couldn't make it, they asked if we wanted to go. We had told them no—why would my older sister and I go to a strange church without them to a seminar we really knew nothing about? But I woke up from that dramatic encounter knowing I was supposed to go. I asked my sister, and she was willing to go as well.

During this seminar, one of the pastors veered the whole thing off of its expected trajectory because he had a word that they were supposed to pray for the youth present. The church had hardly had any youth around because they hadn't focused on it, so the fact that there were over twenty of us that day was a miracle in itself.

My sister and I went up when the pastor said they were going to pray for us. We didn't know what to expect, but a man came and stood in front of me. He had the happiest nature; everything about him beamed and I couldn't wait for him to pray for me, although I hadn't received that kind of ministry from a stranger before.

He smiled and said, "God has shown me that you have been asking big questions and looking for his answers. It's his favorite thing, to have someone ask such big questions, because he can't wait to give you the answers through more relationship with himself. He is putting a hunger for true significance inside of you, and in your lifetime, you will help so many other people really know him. You are going to start hearing his voice. The Spirit of God will come alongside the Word of God that you have been so diligent to read, and you will have your answers!" He prophesied many other things, but those are for a different time.

I just remember feeling so relieved. It was like this man had peeked in on my internal process, and I felt so loved and known. I needed to know God cared more than I did. I needed to know our relationship wasn't one-sided, and not only did God give me an instruction to come to the seminar, he gave that man a word that changed my expectations for life. I was forever changed, and it was so simple.

Picture a teenager in your life who is trying to find his identity and then picture God speaking to him through a stranger. Then picture God saving him because of his kindness and genuine love. That is what the prophetic can do.

THE PROPHETIC WILL SHOW UP IN ALL THE KEY TIMES OF YOUR LIFE, IF YOU ARE OPEN

I love that we are the only people on earth expecting God to lead us. We read the Word for life application. We listen to God's Spirit to really know his desires and will. In this expectation, if we really hear him, it will transform us and then the world around us. I also love that the prophetic allows us go beyond just the knowledge of what is in God's heart for us and others. We don't only hear what he wants to give us, what he made us to do, and whom we get to love; he brings us to understand how to be connected to him in a full way. When we have revelatory experiences, we have the ability to encounter our ageless, timeless God of love and partner with him here on earth.

I spent a season of almost ten years focused solely on the prophetic as my primary ministry, and during that time it was easy to love because there is no catalyst for change in people's lives like revelation. When you have your moment with God, it pulls all the things that are the most important together. It helps you to relate to yourself and the world around you.

THE PROPHETIC IS A RELATIONAL TOOL

When I was growing up, my father was in the Air Force. Because of this we moved many times, and as kids we would dread having to meet new friends and live in new spaces. Before each move my mom would pray with us, and we would ask God to show us things about our new friends. We would ask to hear his voice and see his heart for the community we were going into. I remember one time she had us journal anything we heard. I had seen a few pictures, so I drew out visions and encounters, which God used to prepare me for the new friendships.

I carried this over into my adult years, and the first place I moved to was Kansas City, Missouri. I was worried about moving there because everyone there had grown up together, and I didn't want to be isolated from a community that already shared a lifelong history. I began to ask God about the people, and he prepared my heart and showed me things about some of my future friends. It took the anxiety off of the move, and I couldn't wait to meet the people I was already praying about, even though I only had vague clues about who they were.

We also practiced seeing our friends at the end of the race with the trophy in their hands. This has become an essential skill in friendship, because when you are in times of misunderstanding, or even relational tension, you can still choose to see who the person truly is. When you treat him with that value, it can help you to press through to complete resolution and into a new place of health. How many people stop seeing who their spouse or best friend really is in the midst of conflict and allow brokenness to come in?

I love how hearing from God gives you opportunities you never would have had without his voice.

THE A-LIST ACTOR

I was with an actor-musician one day for lunch. He knew I was a minister but didn't know anything about the prophetic ministry. It was a very nice lunch but very superficial as well. Finally our mutual friend said, "We should all pray together before we go. Why don't you lead, Shawn."

I immediately heard God say, "Tell him to go home and throw away the newspapers he has in the second drawer in his desk; they give an inaccurate report about two different subjects. I have a great report for him, and it's so he can live the John 10:10 abundant life."

I didn't know how he would take this kind of instruction or word, but I had to go past normal nice prayer and tell him. "I feel like God is showing me that there are newspapers in your desk in the second drawer, and he says that they give a false report about two different subjects. You need to throw them away and ask God what his report is."

He turned white. "Do you know what you are saying?" he asked me.

"No, I just heard God say that. He has a great report, but you can't hear it because of the report you keep rereading."

He put his head into his hands and looked very tired. He went from the great actor who gives brilliant performances (and had been giving one all through lunch) to the brokenhearted man who couldn't find a resolution for some secret issues.

"The newspapers deal with two subjects, and I have looked at them every week, sometimes multiple times, for years. The first one is about my father's death. The newspapers reported it was a suicide, and I have always felt something was wrong when I read that report. It was when I was only eight, and my mom always told us that he didn't kill himself, but had gotten involved with an illegal business deal. I never remembered my dad sad, but I have struggled with depression and have always wondered if I could take my own life." He verbally processed. "He didn't kill himself?"

"Obviously not," I replied.

A weight of potential hereditary mental illness came off of his shoulders.

His mother had told him that his father didn't struggle with depression or suicide, but reading the newspaper over and over had opened him up to sadness and depression with lingering suicidal thoughts. The weight of the world came off of him. For some reason, that was the resolution he needed.

The second set of articles, he explained, were reviews on his first two movies. The reviewers had singled him out for being terrible, and no matter how much he worked, he couldn't get their words out of his head. In fact, he rehearsed them every time he reread the articles.

"God has called you to acting; these men are wrong. Maybe your performance was immature, but you are supposed to be an actor, and you have been created to find fulfillment in it as well," I said.

He looked relieved, but not in a human way. He looked as if he was reverse aging. Sorrow and self-pity were draining out of him. By the time we were done praying, he was a new man. After years and years he seemed solid and was doing well career wise, but only God could bring spiritual resolution to the places that he had no natural help for.

I love how the prophetic can restore us in an instant!

In my own life, and in the lives of those I have been privileged to be around, I have had the most amazing relational journey with God. He speaks and gives us hints and understandings on potentially every subject. The Bible proves he is not silent and that he wants to be known and understood. I love how prophecy bridges the gap from his heart to ours and helps us go from small-mindedness to a big picture. It also helps us to live life more fully than we would if it were only up to us and our viewpoints. As you walk with God and he speaks to you, he always talks about whom he loves and what he loves, which gives you an enlarged capacity to experience more.

Many times when I didn't feel qualified, or like I didn't have the relational or emotional capacity, let alone the skillset, to speak to different people (it felt way out of my comfort zone), God's personality and his passion possessed me in a way that made it easy. I am not limited to my resources; I am limited to his, even when reaching outside my comfortable space. The prophetic builds a setting outside of the places our own passions can take us. My life is a 100 percent product of God speaking and leading. He's inspired me to go after heart passions and people I would (absolutely) have never gone after without his voice and nature being made so clear to me. It is a game changer and a life maker to hear from God.

> "I am convinced that the next move of God will bring a marriage between the Word and the Spirit." REVEREND PAUL CAIN

In other words, when we have the Bible and a spiritual walk of relationship with God, the whole world will come under the transformation of God's heart, and with a heart that is that good, who wouldn't want to hear from him?

CHAPTER 4

THE PROPHETIC IS FIRST A CULTURE OF THE HEART

"Men have mystified and philosophized the gospel, but it is as simple as it can be. The secret of Christianity is in being. It is in being a possessor of the nature of Jesus Christ." JOHN G. LAKE

"Follow the way of love and eagerly desire gifts of the Spirit, especially prophecy" (1 Corinthians 14:1 NIV). In this chapter, Paul encourages the Corinthians to follow the way of love or pursue love as the main goal, but also to eagerly desire spiritual gifts, and he highlights the gift of prophecy. The reason why is because prophecy can be one of the clearest validations of the Father's great love, which Jesus paid such a high price for. When people hear the thoughts and emotions of God toward them, they believe in his love for them.

One day I drove to my old favorite coffee house where the rich, famous, wannabees, gonnabees, and has-beens of Hollywood all hang out (it was around the corner from our house), and there was a woman there who was in tatters. Her bad wig was on crooked and showing her own dark roots coming out of the side; her mascara was running longer than the Mississippi; her hands were black and blue; and she looked freezing, even though the morning sun of LA was up, so it wasn't that cold.

Everyone just walked by her, and she was crying in a whisper, "Please, I'm hungry . . . please help me . . . anything . . . I just need food." She was saying this in a very convincing way, but because she had been on the streets so long, she belonged there in passersby's minds. Everyone just rushed by her. She was used to begging, so people were used to ignoring her. She was used to streetwalking, so she was used to being invisible to most people unless they wanted to use her.

Because I have worked in street ministry, I knew she was an old-timer in prostitution, and I knew she must have had one of the worst nights of her life to be there at eight in the morning look-ing somewhat beat up. I walked past her, but at this point she was crumpled in a ball on the ground and crying. I went into Starbucks and ordered two coffees, two breakfast sandwiches, and some other stuff and brought out hands full of food to her. Still, no one was paying any attention to her, because she was one of the lost, for-gotten ones. (Society says, "It's her own fault. Stay away from those types. You can't really help them." And I understand where this comes from, because we aren't trained to help people like her with-out a degree in social work or law enforcement, so people feel pow-erless. It's easier to ignore them.)

I said to her, "Hey, I'm Shawn. What's your name?" and handed her the bags and the coffee.

She looked up at me and stood up. "For me?" She started to take the bags and she hugged me. It was a real hug.

I could see her. . . The world around us just saw this scary, drug-addicted, sick, old prostitute, but somehow I could see her. I could believe in her in that moment and I could see her value. I didn't know what to prophesy and I asked the Father, *What do I say? She is so valuable. . .* And I heard right then four words to say.

I said, right as she gave me the friendly hug: "You are not invisible."

She broke in my arms. Somehow it defined exactly how she felt.

After she cried for a while and I hugged her deeply, she looked into my eyes and said, "Thank you, no one has been kind to me for probably a year."

"Can I do anything else?" I asked.

"You have done more than you could ever know." She hugged me again and I left.

Since then I have seen her on the streets in Hollywood and Silver Lake, and we have had two long talks, initiated by her, about Jesus and his love. She is closer and closer to getting to know him because she sees him all the time now in her life. She sees his goodness and she knows every day, more and more, that he is real. It didn't start for her, though, until she had someone give her more than a word and show her her eternal value.

BEFORE THE PROPHETIC IS A SPIRITUAL GIFT, IT IS A HEART CULTURE

"I died in 1973. My heart stopped. I was brought before Jesus and he only asked me one thing: Did you learn to love, Bob?" BOB JONES

We have to follow love, which is a culture of our heart, more than we should eagerly desire spiritual gifts such as prophecy. "Before you even prophesy out of your mouth there has to be a change in your heart. It starts with really understanding" (John 3:16-17 paraphrased). God loved the whole world so much that he sent Jesus to reconnect to humanity and to his creation. Jesus didn't come to convict the world of what it was doing wrong; he came to put the world back to its right state again—to its connection to God and his original plan. When you start to look around and see everyone as part of this redemptive plan, you begin to fall in love. When Jesus loved the world through his physical form, he didn't come with fragmented thinking about why he was coming. He wasn't in hidden judgement to the world; he was in visible love with it.

> *God knew what he was doing from the very beginning. He decided from the outset to shape the lives of those who love him along the same lines as the life of his Son. The Son stands first in the line of humanity he restored. We see the original and intended shape of our lives there in him. After God made that decision of what his children should be like, he followed it up by calling people by name. After he called them by name, he set them on a solid basis with himself. And then, after getting them established, he stayed with them to the end, gloriously completing what he had begun* (Romans 8:28-29).

I arrived at a conference early and went to one of the other speaker's sessions. I was on a spiritual high because one of my new believer friends had just told me his story that day. He was an entertainment manager, and he had been a drug addict until a year ago, when he radically gave his life to Jesus. During that time his clients shifted, and one of them is one of the most famous pop stars in the world. He finally went to one of her concerts to reconnect to his old world and just say "hello" again after a whole year, and afterwards he was invited into the backstage party. There were a lot of drugs, but the pop star invited him over to a more private seating area.

"What is going on?" she asked. "You are usually in the middle of the party," implying he wasn't using drugs. "What's up?" She challenged him with a smile.

She wasn't using either, and he noticed that.

"This is going to sound cliché, but I met Jesus. I have been sober a year and am the happiest I ever have been."

She smiled. "I knew something profound happened. You have to tell me all about your journey!"

He was so surprised she wanted to hear his whole testimony and about all the changes he had gone through since becoming a Christian. He related how easy it was to protect his love for God, himself, and his family now that he was a Christian, and drugs were off the table for him forever.

"This is the most real spiritual pursuit story I have ever heard!" she declared. "I am not ready to become a Christian, but will you pray with me that I have an encounter with God in a real way like you have?"

They prayed and cried together. It was a beautiful seed planted.

So fast-forward to the conference with a very well-known speaker (that I didn't know personally). I went to his session to get to know him, and you know what? He was amazing . . . except for one thing. He said, "There is this very well-known pop singer, you know her name [he named her]. She is responsible for immorality in the younger generation and God is going to judge her." Immediately I disengaged from his entire service and was screaming *NOOOOOO!* in my heart. I wanted to jump up and say, "She just doesn't know the love of God; don't talk about her, because she is close, and if she heard what you were saying, she would think God hates her, because you do!"

YOU WILL NEVER HAVE AUTHORITY OVER WHAT YOU DO NOT LOVE

And right then I heard the sadness in the Father's heart as he said, "You will never have any authority over what you do not love. This minister doesn't know that I want to give him, and others, authority to go to these public figures in love, but they have a huge problem when they separate their love from them. To him she is an untouchable person. He doesn't realize that she might hear this at some point in her pursuit of me. He doesn't realize that even mentioning her name could cause her ears to perk up, but he is too far removed from her to really care. To you, I want you to expect me to send you (and the people you love) to them, because I want to reach them. I will give you authority to connect to them if you will let my love have authority in your heart."

I was so happy for what he was inviting me into, but so sad that the speaker represented so many Christians who don't believe they or their friends and family will have authority to speak to presidents, pop stars, local authorities, or anyone of prominence. If we believe God loves them too, why wouldn't he send us? God wouldn't have had the authority to inherit us if he didn't love us. He does not hate anyone alive, and the first part of moving in the prophetic is to start embracing the culture of his loving heart and living that way. This love is the landing strip to seeing his thoughts and intentions toward humanity. If you are against people and countries and industries, where is the highest revelation of his heart supposed to land?

If I speak against popular pop stars or movies stars or presidents, how can God send me to them with his voice when there is no honor, no love, no compassion, no kindness? These are all the things present in a heart culture of love that is already prophetic, even before it prophesies with the tools of prophecy. You cannot be a continually prophetic voice if you are in conflict with the world that God loves. Think about it: if they heard you speak against them, they would never want to hear from you. In a world where you can do Twitter or Google searches for your name and everything that anyone says about you comes up, don't you think we need to guard our mouths and hearts? If you are against them, you have already set up a wall to the process of love just by having a negative opinion.

"True prophetic ministry looks for the gold in the midst of the dirt of people's lives." KRIS VALOTTON

THE PHONE CALL

One day I was processing with an assistant about a celebrity (in the entertainment industry) who had recently come to Christ but still seemed very confused and messy. He asked if I believed the celebrity was even saved, and I was about to be negative when instead I said, "You know what, he has so many choices he can make that if he is publically pronouncing Christ, I just want to give him the benefit of the doubt and believe for God to do a complete work in his life. I want to be so openhearted that if he called right now, I could be relevant in my belief and love for him."

And you know what? Right at that minute I got an unlisted phone call. I answered it and it was him! It's like God was testing my resolve to love and entrusting me with his friend right then. When I firsthand heard his story, it was beautiful and full of redemption. He had come out of more than most people I have ever known, and yet he was more than a survivor. He had remade his life and now he was ready to let God have it.

There is no power from God that is separated from love. If you want to have influence, you have to join yourself to his love nature. This is more than a feeling or an emotion. It is an attitude of acceptance toward everyone and everything that is God's, even if you can't control it, manage it, or even nurture it. You are called to love.

TAKING ON THE DIVINE NATURE OF CHRIST

You can't show this value to someone just by words or by human compassion. It has to come out of your character, emotions, thoughts, and spirit—your nature empowered by God's very nature. Second Peter 1:3-4 says that we get to participate with the divine nature of Christ. The essence of prophecy is the very nature of Jesus being imparted into a human being. This is one of the strongest statements in Scripture: We participate with the actual nature of Jesus. A nature is the sum of personality, emotions, character, spirit, and talents that make up an individual. Our nature is what defines each one of us. The Scripture here, and several others, says that while we are in relationship with God, we participate with his nature.

We cannot limit ourselves and our understanding of God. Participating with his nature means we are not limited to our weakness or strengths, our personality, our gifts, our talents, or our emotions. We have a living God who has all of these strengths that we are relating to too. The nature of the supernatural does not depend on the nature, skill, gifting, or calling of man but on the actual supernatural love of God being imparted to us, the vessels of his honor. When you are partnering with this nature, you will make decisions that don't always seem like yours. You will go places and talk to people and do things that are not limited to your rational thinking or your life experiences. You will also do things out of his goodness and have an instinct for what will make the world better.

WE HAVE TO HAVE EVERYONE'S BEST INTEREST AT HEART

I have realized that most of us can speak negatively about our president, about pop idols, about other religions, etc. because we don't have authority. When you have authority, you will realize that those people you speak about will hear you and be hurt or shut you off based on what you say. Part of the heart culture that we have to have is in the truth that everyone is worthy. We need to have a heart to love first, because God might just use us to win one of the enemies of Christianity to his cause.

I want to be like Barnabas. When Paul got saved, he fought for him in the midst of a Christian culture that had written him off because of his past offenses. The prophetic sees people in their full value, and when there is so much passion in God's heart for them, our hearts have a hard time focusing on the negative in them. We grow in authority to reach people of authority by seeing God's value of them and seeing them as worthy.

"He who gives the most hope will have the greatest influence." KRIS VALOTTON

LIFE IN THE SPIRIT—FRUIT CHECK

Galatians 5 describes the fruit of a life in the Spirit, and it is an extremely accurate measure of how you are governing your heart when you are carrying the nature of God. If you need a list of rules for how to govern your prophetic gifting, read on.

But what happens when we live God's way? He brings gifts into our lives, much the same way that fruit appears in an orchard—things like affection for others, exuberance about life, serenity. We develop a willingness to stick with things, a sense of compassion in the heart, and a conviction that a

basic holiness permeates things and people. We find ourselves involved in loyal commitments, not needing to force our way in life, able to marshal and direct our energies wisely.

Legalism is helpless in bringing this about; it only gets in the way. Among those who belong to Christ, everything connected with getting our own way and mindlessly responding to what everyone else calls necessities is killed off for good— crucified.

Since this is the kind of life we have chosen, the life of the Spirit, let us make sure that we do not just hold it as an idea in our heads or a sentiment in our hearts, but work out its implications in every detail of our lives. That means we will not compare ourselves with each other as if one of us were better and another worse. We have far more interesting things to do with our lives. Each of us is an original (Galatians 5:22-26).

A CONVICTION THAT BASIC HOLINESS PERMEATES THINGS AND PEOPLE

As we focus on a life of love through Christ, there has to be a basic culture in our hearts that believes the best about his plans for humanity. This doesn't mean we put a positive spin on everything, but we do have to have the heart quality that believes God is everywhere and he wants to bring everything into his heart. Everyone who is still living is worthy of this love.

When we go after a heart culture of living a life in the Spirit, we have the fruit of a life in God that is clearly laid out in Galatians. This seems to be the most needed installment in those who pursue the prophetic as a lifestyle or ministry.

Let's set the standard of love and lifestyle really high in this generation!

THE DICTATOR OF A SOUTH AMERICAN COUNTRY

One of my trips down to South America was very eye-opening to me. I met a man who worked as an intern in the government of the country I was in, and he came to me and said, "My relative is a president, and I want you to meet him and share what God is showing you about our country." It was a different country than I was in, but we were bordering it and we could get there on a quick helicopter ride.

I didn't have anything for the president, nor was I familiar enough with his country to know anything, so I asked the host pastors about him and his country, and they told me how awful he was. They showed me article after online article about this tyrant and warlord. . .

I didn't want to meet with him. I was going to meet back up with his relative later on that night and explain why this was not a good idea. I took a nap that afternoon and had a dream. In the dream, I saw this little boy of about twelve years old caught up in the foster care system. He had never had good parenting and he had been thrown around. I watched his life and saw his heart, and I had more and more compassion for him as the dream played out. I so wanted to reach out to him and tell him it was going to be okay. In the dream he ended up leading the orphanage he was in, and I was so sad. I heard God say, "Will you be a father to him for a minute?" as I woke up.

I knew this was a dream about this president. I had a new sense of human compassion and love in my heart for him and wanted to meet with him. He was leading a whole nation of orphans with the mentality of an orphan. This was not a meeting to endorse his presidency or calling over his nation; this was a rescue mission for his heart. I began to pray and heard two very important things, but I didn't know what they meant.

I ended up flying to him later that day. I had an armed escort that reminded me of an '80s action movie, but I knew they were not there to protect me; they were there for him. When they brought me to him, it was a very powerful scene. This man commanded respect, and he had such an air of hardness that I almost wanted to turn around right there.

"Hello," I said as I stuck my hand out to greet him. He was suspicious and looked at his relative with almost disdain.

"Yes, you are here to pray," he said in pretty perfect English.

I didn't know if I was going to need an interpreter or not. "What will you pray for, man of God?" He didn't ask in a mocking way, but I knew he was just doing a favor for his relative.

"I actually want you to know, as a Christian, that God loves you and has put a love in my heart for you, and I really do want to pray from that place of love. He told me two things." For some reason I could feel his heart warm up, but at the same time there was no belief in him towards me.

"What did he tell you?" He appeared very amused.

"He told me that he wouldn't help you with this [phrase withheld]." It was like a five-word code name.

Two men behind him breathed in when I said it, and he told everyone to get out of the room other than those two men, myself, and one heavily armed soldier. Even his relative left. I should have been nervous, but I wasn't.

"How do you know this?" he asked.

"I know nothing but what God told me," I said. "He also told me that he already forgave you for what happened with your daughter with the horse when she was eight at her birthday party, and you don't have to ask him to forgive you anymore." I won't write what he did, but it was such a picture of his orphan nature.

He got tears in his eyes. He sat down, so I sat down. He hunched over for a minute. "I don't know if I believe God could forgive me. I ask forgiveness for my sins against my family every day to God."

"I didn't think so either, but when I prayed for you, he showed me how much he still loves you and how much he wants you to know him as a father. He is not like your father was, and you are not like your son." He began to cry. The two men who were still in the room were probably generals or his council. They looked embarrassed and worried for him.

"I will not do the first thing that you mentioned if God is not with me. It was a war effort. There are too many politics to go into, but that was our code name for it. As for God loving me as a father, pray for me, because I don't know this kind of love."

He didn't know I would take him literally. I closed my eyes and prayed for him. When I was finished, he shook my hands and then embraced me. Everyone looked shocked. Then he sent me off but tried to give me money. I refused it and told him God wouldn't have sent me there to get something; it was for his benefit to receive.

His relative and I talked and he filled me in on the big picture of the story. I have never talked about it again publically, even with this much detail, even though he has passed away now. I just know that God gave me a heart of love for this dictator who was continually corrupt and who had no redemptive value outside the cross. I felt like this could be a good picture for you, the reader, to know that God will use the prophetic to get to anyone alive to receive his love, even if for only a minute. This dictator felt the love of God and hope in the midst of a terrible career and life. God wants to love through you too.

PAUL CAIN AND SADAM HUSSEIN

Paul Cain has been a personal friend and mentor to me. He is a prophet most notably known by the '50s' healing and evangelism ministries and also from the 1980s-1990s' Vineyard prophetic movement. His stories have always been an inspiration to me. At one point during the Middle East crisis, God gave him such an accurate word for Saddam Hussein that he was invited to see him. We believe he was the only non-governmental American to visit Saddam in that season.

When they met, Paul prophesied powerfully over him and was filled with spiritual respect for him (which means he didn't have any natural respect for this dictator or how he ruled, but he had redemptive love in his heart for him). Saddam didn't get saved when Paul came to him on two different trips; he was fully empowered in his evil regime and way too arrogant. But I think about him when he was like Nebuchadnezzar—in the pit in the end of his life—and I wonder if he looked for God and replayed the words of Paul in his heart or head as he was nearing his death. God so loved the whole world, even an evil dictator, that he sent Paul Cain.

CAN GOD SEND YOU?

Who does God love that he wants to send you to? Will you be willing to go? Will you obey him with those around you first so he can entrust you with the hardest or the best later?

CHAPTER 5

THE NATURE OF NEW TESTAMENT REVELATION

We are becoming something that is beyond what we could be if we were limited to our own gifts, talents, and nature. When we have Jesus living inside of us through his Spirit, we get to participate with his thoughts, his favor, and his design, and we see greater fruit in our lives.

The spirit of revelation that the Bible and people refer to is the Holy Spirit bringing revelation of all that God wants to do, and who God is, so as to fulfill everything that needs to happen for Jesus to have his prepared bride.

GOD'S HEART AND MIND ARE GIVEN THROUGH THE PROPHETIC AND GIVE US COURAGE TO "BECOME"

"Where there is no revelation people cast off restraint, but blessed is he who keeps the commands" (Proverbs 29:18). In other words, revelation brings about the right order of purpose. The feeling of being totally synchronized, whether in sports, the arts, or a job (or even just healthy relational order) is very similar to what revelation helps promote in our lives. It keeps us feeling extremely connected to ourselves and the world around us. It keeps us willing to sacrifice and live morally, because we have seen God in a relational way that makes us want to protect our relationship at all costs.

Another way to say it is that the spirit of revelation is basically God's Spirit keeping us connected to his thoughts and heart for us and his Son. It's when the person and nature of God manifests to our understanding, spirit, and emotions. Paul prayed over Ephesus: "I keep asking that the God of our Lord Jesus Christ, the glorious Father, may give you the Spirit of wisdom and revelation, so that you may know him better" (Ephesians 1:17-19 NIV). What a profoundly simple prayer. He wasn't praying for believers to have wisdom and revelation so they could perform in their Christianity better, or so they could dominate the world. He prayed it with a simple core focus of Christianity's basic belief system: May you have revelation to really know Jesus.

This is what John saw (see Revelation 1) when he had the revelation of Jesus. God's great desire is to share his identity and his nature with us. He wants us to know and have his love, his purpose, and his agenda so we can partner with him and be driven by what drives him.

OLD TESTAMENT VS. NEW TESTAMENT UNDERSTANDING OF PROPHECY

When you look at the Old Testament, it is a book about God pursuing and wooing his people, the Jews, back into connection with him. He is faithful to lead them, speak to them, and love them, but he does so in a very different way than he does in the New Testament. Contrasting the way prophecy functions in the Old Testament versus the way it does in the New Testament is important. The main contrast is in who God used and how he used them. God would select someone who had a very special nature and destiny that was rare to his generation. God would put his leadership on him and speak to only him, or a few, in one generation in order to lead his people.

These chosen prophets were extremely close to God's heart, and he treated them as friends. Some were even a picture of the relationship we get to experience now as Christians. Each prophet had to be extremely careful, because he was the only steward of God's desire on the earth in his day. These kings, judges, prophets, and leaders were responsible for shepherding all of God's chosen people. If they didn't speak when God showed them something, then all of God's people could be misled. If the people didn't listen, then God would have to discipline them. To understand this fully would take a whole Bible course, but it's worth the study!

WE ARE JUSTIFIED BY OUR OWN FAITH IN GOD. NO ONE CAN EARN IT FOR US

In the Old Testament, prophecy was about obedience to the Lord through his chosen servants. You didn't necessarily have your own word on a matter, but were waiting to hear what God spoke to your king, prophet, or leader. In the Atonement (New Testament times to today), each believer has a connection to the Spirit of God because of the price Jesus paid. We are each being justified by our own faith in God. No one can make the decision of salvation or relationship with God for us. We each must have our own connection, so in the New Testament you see believers who are empowering this relationship and spreading it. They are displaying signs and wonders, miracles, and speaking for God through his Spirit as a Christian community.

JESUS PROMISED THAT GOD WOULD SPEAK TO EVERY BELIEVER

Jesus was constantly pointing out that God wants to speak to each believer, and illustrated it with the parable of the good shepherd who speaks to his sheep (see John 10). He even promised that all those with him would have the Holy Spirit to the same measure he did so they could hear the Father just as intimately (see John 16). "But when he, the Spirit of truth, comes, he will guide you into all the truth. He will not speak on his own; he will speak only what he hears, and he will tell you what is yet to come. He will glorify me because it is from me that he will receive what he will make known to you. All that belongs to the Father is mine. That is why I said the Spirit will receive from me what he will make known to you" (John 16:13 NIV).

This is a completely different connection to God that the Jews didn't have (before the Atonement), even though it was God's original plan to have us intimately connected, as when Adam and Eve went walking with God in the garden.

BEING PERSONALLY LED BY GOD

In the Old Testament, a prophet was the spiritual leader of the nation and, for the most part, God did not move without revealing his plans to a prophet first. This was very important, because God was showing that he would guard and nurture his covenant with the Jewish people until he restored them. He did this through his chosen servants, whom he raised up out of terrible odds. They were to lead in a way that would make it obvious to everyone in the world (or at least the Jews) that they were chosen. They were a sign and a wonder to a whole generation, leading their people into exactly what God promised and protecting their people from all the enemies of God, including those amongst themselves.

In the New Testament, however, every single believer was given the responsibility for his own spiritual journey and growth with God, and his walk was not to be independent of a body of believers or community. Every single person who believes becomes a signpost to the kingdom of God and a sign of the promise that Jesus will return again to those who love him. The message has since gone everywhere in the world. Kingdom government is not a system or an anointed man; it's a government of God's love and Spirit guiding people as they interpret the Bible together for the days and time they live in. Instead of God only leading Israel into its specific promises, he includes everyone (through salvation). So although there are still very important promises and purposes on the Jewish people that we need to treasure and look forward to, the Spirit of God is on all of humanity so that all will be restored to his full grace.

JUSTIFIED BY FAITH

When Martin Luther nailed his thesis to the Wittenberg door, he was fighting for all to have the right to know that we are all justified before God by our *own* faith in God. In other words, we have an individual responsibility to hear God and interpret his Word. We are not going to heaven or living a full life just because we have the leadership of church in our lives; we have a personal responsibility to hear God through the Word and the Spirit on our own time. In other words, we can't live vicariously through the church, a prophet, or an institution's sanctity; we have to be sanctified and set apart in our own relationship with God.

That is why prophecy should be encouraging, comforting, and edifying, because God is already speaking in our core being, and prophecy should validate what we already know about empowering through love. It doesn't mean our prophetic words won't have new direction or connection, but prophecy isn't supposed to have the goal of being directive in a commanding way. It should leave room for the persons receiving the word to be accountable to God themselves for their choices, *not demanding this choice be made for them.*

The Bible is a spiritual guide that must be followed. Everything we need from God to live a successful Christian life is found there, and we have the Spirit to guide this living journey of relationship. The Bible becomes the only ultimate authority in God's directive voice over our lives, so if someone tells you to move because God has told him you will not thrive in your city and it *doesn't* feel like God himself is asking you to move, you don't have to. The Bible isn't telling you to move, and neither is the Spirit. There will be no negative consequences to following God, but there may be for following man. Certain Christian communities treat the voice of the prophet and the authority of the Bible as the same thing, and sometimes they just aren't even connected.

Prophecy from others should never violate our will or ability to have choices. So many people who have moved in the prophetic in modern times have patterned themselves after an Old Testament prophet and are trying to lead their churches or movements by old rules, rules that just don't have the atonement and restoration of relationship to God in their theologies. This can cause devastating control and manipulation of the flock, because when you think God has spoken and you use what you hear to direct and lead people in ways they wouldn't normally go, you are violating their own faith journeys with God.

The world doesn't need another Holy Spirit or another Jesus; it needs the connection to the One it already has.

Anyone trying to substitute himself into this role will find himself to be a very legalistic and unfulfilling leader.

NOT ABOUT INFORMATION BUT ABOUT RELATIONSHIP

In the Old Testament, God led Israel with prophets who were infallible (for the most part). If they weren't, they were put to death for being wrong or misleading. There are numerous Scriptures about God investing his love in his people by speaking through one of his chosen vessels. He asked his covenant people, the Jews, to be completely honoring of this so they would not only live and be fruitful, but also so they would come into the full prosperity of their purpose as a people group. God spoke in commands and decrees so that through their traditions and obedience, they could come into an understanding of his love and covenant.

When Jesus came as the complete fulfillment of all that was promised to the Jewish people (regarding a Messiah), he connected them directly to God. After Paul, the greatest apostle, had his encounter on the road to Damascus, he had a revelation of biblical proportions. The Gentiles (everyone not Jewish) were also benefactors of this great fulfillment. The whole world had atonement for its broken relationship with God, and now we can all build a relationship directly with the Father, through the Spirit of God, because of what Jesus did on the cross.

The New Testament doesn't highlight information or accuracy when God speaks; it highlights love. As Paul says: "The only thing that counts is faith expressing itself through love" (Galatians 5:6b NIV). The New Testament emphasizes our reception of the power of the Spirit, together with all other believers. The disciples received the same abiding or resting presence on them (see Acts 2:1-4) that Jesus did when he received the anointing through John the Baptist. The presence of God was the disciples' first manifest answer to the prayer of Jesus to his Father before he was betrayed (see John 17).

In response to this manifestation, Peter quoted Joel 2 and said that the Spirit of God was on them and that their young men were seeing visions and their old men were having dreams. In other words, God's Spirit was (and is) on everyone, and they were all being prophetic because God had restored his relationship with humanity through Jesus Christ.

This means that the goal and jurisdiction of prophecy is not to give us information on how God is leading us into covenant or away from our sins. The primary purpose of the Spirit's words is to reveal the love of our Father and our relationship with him. Since we are all able to hear from God for ourselves, our goal in hearing from God for each other is to encourage that love relationship and affirm that great connection. God is no longer leading his people toward that connection. It has been made and freely given, even to non-Jews, so now we can rest in building that relationship instead of living vicariously through others who have it.

There are still very specific prophecies for the Jewish people who God put his very heart in. We respect these special revelations that in the end will prove God's full redemptive plan.

PAUL KNEW GOD WAS CALLING HIM TO ROME AND A PROPHET TRIED TO STOP HIM

This was seen clearly when Agabus went to Paul and begged him not to go to Rome because he had revelation that Paul would be imprisoned. Here is the story:

After we had been there a number of days, a prophet named Agabus came down from Judea. Coming over to us, he took Paul's belt, tied his own hands and feet with it and said, "The Holy Spirit says, 'In this way the Jewish leaders in Jerusalem will bind the owner of this belt and will hand him over to the Gentiles.'"

When we heard this, we and the people there pleaded with Paul not to go up to Jerusalem. Then Paul answered, "Why are you weeping and breaking my heart? I am ready not only to be bound, but also to die in Jerusalem for the name of the Lord Jesus." When he would not be dissuaded, we gave up and said, "The Lord's will be done" (Acts 21:10-14 NIV).

Three important facts are here in dealing with New Testament believers:

1) When you study what happened to Paul, Agabus actually had one of his details wrong. The Gentiles actually rescued Paul from the Jews because he was a respected Roman citizen, while Agabus had implied that the Gentiles would kill him.

2) Paul had already heard from God that he was supposed to go to Rome, so even one of the prophets couldn't convince him otherwise.

3) Agabus was never called a false prophet for either of these facts, but was dearly loved by all.

This shows you, from one of the only stories of a prophet in the New Testament, how far things had changed (because of the Spirit of God that is upon each believer). It is not about information or direction; it is about growing in connection and relationship with God. Agabus had discerned something, and he may have even sensed something from the heart of God, but his thoughts and revelation were incomplete compared to Paul's.

IT'S NOT JUST ABOUT INFORMATION ANYMORE; IT'S ABOUT LOVE

I was at a well-known coffee place in Hollywood, and I saw a guy in line who I knew was in the entertainment industry. I felt drawn to him and so began to ask God to share his heart with me so I could talk to him.

I went up to him and asked, "Hey, do you have a brother named Stephan? Or a cousin?"

He smiled at me and said no questioningly.

I said thanks and began to hightail it away, feeling embarrassed that my word of knowledge didn't go anywhere.

"Wait!" he said. "Why did you ask?"

I knew I had a few choices. I could make it sound like I thought I knew his brother/cousin. I could say there was no reason. I could ignore him. But I felt responsible to be honest.

"It's funny, actually. I am practicing hearing God's voice, and that's why I asked you. I thought God showed me something." I braced myself for the rejection that would come with such a weird response.

"Oh my gosh, I have been waiting my whole life to talk to someone who hears the voice of God! Do you have time to sit down and explain that to me?" He was ecstatic!

You know what? He got saved after forty-five minutes from what started out to be a wrong word of knowledge. Information *doesn't* matter; love *does*. Love covers even when we are wrong, because relationship bridges gaps that risks or even immaturity create.

GOD IS OPENING OUR EARS AND EYES AND GIVING US HIS MIND

Another one of my favorite distinctions is when Paul describes what our relationship with the Holy Spirit does for us, which is foundational to our Christian experience:

However, as it is written: "What no eye has seen, what no ear has heard, and what no human mind has conceived"— the things God has prepared for those who love him—these are the things God has revealed to us by his Spirit.

The Spirit searches all things, even the deep things of God. For who knows a person's thoughts except their own spirit within them? In the same way no one knows the thoughts of God except the Spirit of God. What we have received is not the spirit of the world, but the Spirit who is from God, so that we may understand what God has freely given us. This is what we speak, not in words taught us by human wisdom but in words taught by the Spirit, explaining spiritual realities with Spirit-taught words. The person without the Spirit does not accept the things that come from the Spirit of God but considers them foolishness, and cannot understand them because they are discerned only through the Spirit. The person with the Spirit makes judgments about all things, but such a person is not subject to merely human judgments, for, "Who has known the mind of the Lord so as to instruct him?" (1 Corinthians 2:9).

In the Old Testament, God was tying the Jewish people to the fact that he wanted to open their eyes and ears again. He wanted to give them his mind so they could be connected to him the way they were designed to. He was constantly helping them see where their eyes were closed and their ears deaf so that they could have hope for a full revelation or understanding. He rebuked the Israelites for trying to say they had his mind (the mind of God) when they were speaking for themselves. He set the goal of what restoration to the fullness of his kingdom looks like so high that he chastised them and loved them even when they went radically astray.

Paul addressed the difference between those who came before Jesus's resurrection and after it. He said, "We have it!" In other words, no one had *had* the mind of the Lord, but Paul said that we *have* God's mind, thanks to our very deep connection with the Spirit of God. God speaks his thoughts into our deep places.

BOB JONES AND THE PROPHECY TO AVOID LOS ANGELES

Bob Jones was like a grandfather to me. He had such a prejudice (based on some of his earlier spiritual visions) about California that when I told him I was finally going to move there, he begged me not to go. He was convinced that the big earthquake was coming and that not even prayer could hold it back. He even prophesied a few times it would happen, along with dates and timeframes.

I explained to him, "Bob, I have to be able to reject your word without rejecting you and vice versa. I need you, and just because I don't believe in your word over California, no matter how passionate you are, it doesn't mean I don't trust you in so many other areas. Can you stay connected to me, even though I am not trusting your spiritual perspective and think it's a little crazy?"

He smiled and said "yes." This was a mark of a true New Testament prophet; it was about love, not about the information or word.

Years later he gave me two key prophecies about California—he said a revival would come through TV and film, and he prayed that I would "tell a vision" through TV and film, and you know what? WE ARE! Thank God for the prophetic.

CHAPTER 6

REVELATION—A STEP PAST DISCERNMENT

REVELATION CAUSES US TO DISCERN GOD'S MIND AND DEEP HEART

"Who, while walking in the prophetic and when meeting people, first sees or senses the negative people are dealing with? If you do, it's because God is trusting you with his heart and asking you to speak the opposite. He wants you to call the gold out of them!" GRAHAM COOKE

Humanity is hardwired for discernment. We are born with intuition, and God created us with the ability to discern each other's motives, hearts, gifts, talents, and skills. As we pray, it's easy to discern, feel, or sense things about the things we are praying about. This is a wonderful ability God made us with. It's a relational tool, but it is not a substitute for relationship itself.

When you discern things, you're not necessarily getting a prophetic message of revelation. It's more of a conversation starter. It's God helping your spirit man use your spiritual eyes and feelings to know and glimpse the world around you. It's all the senses plus your spiritual senses working together, and they are God's gifts of connection to you. Connect with God first and allow your discernment to be the door for spiritual revelation that goes beyond your thoughts, feelings, opinions, or faith. God wants you to take what you discern and talk to him about it. Then he can reveal his deep heart and share his thoughts about it.

I've come to believe that a lot of words given by a "prophet" are just words of discernment, nothing more, because the giver of the word has not gone beyond his own mind and heart and traveled into God's. That takes connection. Anyone can discern something if he listens up for a moment, but only Christians can consistently pursue the heart of God through his Spirit and hear what he is saying *about* their discernment.

A HUGE SEGMENT OF CHRISTIAN LEADERS ARE DISCERN-ING WITHOUT FOLLOWING THROUGH WITH PROPHETIC WORDS

Our LA example: If you type "Los Angeles Prophecy" into a search engine, you will find hundreds of pages of people claiming it will be destroyed and that tsunamis and earthquakes are coming to judge it. It's hard to find a positive word because the world has so much generational offense against Southern California. Remember, even Bob Jones, whom I respected and trusted above all the prophetic people in my life, had a bad thing to say about California.

For Americans, part of it is that there has always been both negative and positive attention on California. The negative perception on California was present from its beginning, alongside a thrilling reputation that anyone might be able to have a better life there. Whether it was the gold rush, the entertainment industry, or the business industries birthed there, there have always been dreamers leaving their families and communities to try out California's promise that big dreams may come true. Unfortunately, many family members watched a loved one who left for the gold rush die (one out of every five members of families). They saw only a small percentage of people who went after the entertainment industry make it. They saw pain and suffering, and every time they heard of failed businesses, it added to the stigma California had already earned itself.

Christianity has had some of the greatest moves of God come directly out of California, but also some of the worst moral discretions—from Christian leaders to Christian cults to unbalanced Christian-focused media. Southern California was the Wild West of the church for a while. Discerning what is wrong with California is easy. Discerning what is right is a little harder, but not that difficult. Discerning God's heart for what he wants for California only comes by revelation and intimacy. Many people have assumed that because so many revivals have come out of California, we are assured a revival from there again. Some people assume, in their faith-based perspective, that because so much evil has come out of California, we are doomed in the long term.

Both of these assumptions can be birthed out of deep presumption. I know what God wants because I have read about him; I have heard what he has done before and will do again; I have deep knowledge of his principles; I have seen him act throughout biblical history, etc.

The reality is that knowledge that is not married to love and spiritual awareness can become religious. Paul found this out when he was on the road to Damascus. He was one of the most educated men in the whole Jewish culture, yet he used knowledge to violate the very God he thought he was passionate about. He had a disconnection and presumption based on his natural discernment, wisdom, education, and his culture's state of religion. We are at risk to have this same presumption enter our hearts when we don't put love first. We can't keep our perspective if it's based only on what we can discern in our natural mind or understanding.

When we came to California, we had people join us who were so offended that anyone would pronounce God's judgement on California that they overcompensated on grace, saying, "Everything is okay, God loves us, there is nothing wrong." Then we had people on the outside saying, "See? You have a convoluted theology of grace! God has to judge sin!"

The balance we need comes from knowing that we are supposed to be like Jesus, who came to God's beloved world as an explanation of that love. John 3:17 says Jesus didn't come into the world to convict it of sin, because that's the Holy Spirit's job. We get to come in loving the world, showing people who they are, and helping them to see the safe boundaries around that revelation. When people see who God is and what he wants, and if they want to be connected to God, they will protect that connection at all costs once they experience it. However, if we start out not giving a revelation of who God is but only giving the principles of his kingdom, then people will never come into (or want to come into) a place of relationship with him.

Holiness is not sinlessness; it is the ability to see what is worth protecting and then say no to sin to protect our yes to love. When we understand this, we can be the prophetic people we were designed to be without being judgment prophets, proclaiming people must change to inherit relationship with God. We become models and spokesmen pointing out how to get more connected to God's love. Then we can model how to stay connected by getting rid of various patterns that stop that connection and relationship.

It appears that even Jesus's followers on the earth couldn't remain sinless. They all failed, but they knew how to protect their connection (or reconnection) with God.

I ONLY NEED ONE HOLY SPIRIT, SHAWN

I went through, like most people who become church-going Christians, a radical religious phase. Mine was when I was a teen-ager, which is a double whammy, because many teens think they already know everything. Put some religious pride and a desire to have awesome supernatural impact through prophecy onto that, and your family will suffer. I remember over-spiritualizing everything, and one day, after trying to convict my mom of something that wasn't even sin but was something I didn't like, she turned around and looked at me and said, "I ONLY NEED ONE HOLY SPIRIT, SHAWN!"

This deeply penetrated my heart, because I was not trying to be like Jesus by loving and encouraging humanity. I was trying to change the world around me by convicting it, hoping that if it got better, I would be happier. The people who use their religion to police the world around them become some of the most unhappy and dangerous people on earth.

No one needs the prophetic to point out where he is failing. We all know we are weak. We don't need a good shaming to get better. We need hope and life. Jesus was *never* motivated to use revelation to shame anyone. He was *always* motivated to use revelation to build all individuals he encountered a framework of heaven's heart and love for them. He often spent time with people who were easy to judge, and he invited them to a place of spiritual importance through his investment in them.

PROPHECY OF EARTHQUAKES IN PERU

I woke up on February 1, 2001, and heard God say, "An earthquake is coming in June to Peru and will destroy many buildings and houses. The enemy knows this and wants to capitalize on it by killing thousands. Tell the churches in Peru to get ready, buy insurance, and help their people to be earthquake proof."

I knew one of the larger churches outside of Lima, so I called the pastor and told him this. Then he asked me what days, and I saw a coverage from June 23-28 and said, "I don't know the exact day, but I know that God wants to spare people and help them in your town and others."

I had given this pastor and a few others some very specific words in the past, and their hearts were open to consider this one because of my track record. As they went to their church and friends' churches with the possibility of the earthquake, they all agreed it would be good to buy earthquake insurance for the churches, businesses, houses, etc. for anyone they could. Many people earthquake proofed even their houses. One of the most amazing things they did is they hosted a citywide multi-church gathering of consecration and prayer, which ran for seven days up in the mountains during the dates I had given him. Over one thousand people went either each day or stayed for the entire time.

On June 24, the earthquake hit and devastated the country, but because these churches were praying beforehand, the death toll was minimal and the injuries were not in the tens of thousands (although over 1700 were injured). They knew that God had protected their nation, and they felt so valued and loved by God. Not only that, but many of these believers benefited in a great way—they were able to rebuild their houses and businesses, and even turn the churches into beautiful earthquake-proof structures, because of the insurance money. My pastor friend asked me to come down in 2005 to see the rebuild, and when I did it was beautiful—much nicer than the church I belonged to in the States!

GOD WANTS TO REVEAL HARD THINGS, NOT JUST HAPPY THINGS, BUT IT'S ALWAYS FOR GOODNESS

"Faith doesn't deny a problem's existence. It denies it a place of influence." BILL JOHNSON

God helped that whole community relate to a very devastating event by showing he was good. Some were affected negatively, but they could see how God helped many, and they were also able to hear the church's message of how God could now dispense good in the midst of the devil's plans for evil. The church's reaction was a great example of kingdom people who become a resource for their community in times of tragedy, because the Peruvian church became a distribution center for aid. They were prepared.

Most messages that come from charismatic and Pentecostal voices after tragedy are: *You deserved this! Your sin brought this upon you! You are unworthy and God hates you, so you were judged!* This is an anti-Jesus message. He came to the whole world because even though it was in a dark place, he willingly considered everyone worthy of the price he would pay on the cross. He knew about the child brothels in Rome, he knew about the slavery in every nation, he knew about the Jewish people embezzling money from the temple, he knew all about temple prostitutes and rampant sexual immorality. He came into that time for the people of that time and was not offended. Instead he was willing to say: "You are worth my price!"

He would have never died on the cross with the theology in his heart that most Christians have today. As a matter of fact, some current Christians wouldn't be happy with their city or any other, even if Jesus died for it again, meaning they don't think his price has enough value for the sin in their regions. They live as if there is still a curse that can negate God's love.

BAD THEOLOGY = JUDGEMENT AND NEGATIVE PROPHE-CY

When we are affected negatively by some sin in our family or community, we often try and have a spiritual perspective on what is going on, but if we stay in discernment alone and add negative theology or eschatology, then we will prophesy a wiping clean of the slate before God can start again. "God has to judge this so he can clean it up" (which is never a New Testament theology). Referencing John 3:17 again: It says Jesus didn't come to be judgmental over worldly issues, but to pay a price to bring God's original design and purpose back to the world. When we speak over the world what it is supposed to be, we give it an opportunity to be transformed instead of destroyed.

One of the most beautiful parts of embracing Christ is that he delivers us from having to reap what we have sown. It doesn't mean that there are no consequences for choices, but he stops vicious cycles in our lives when we repent and return to him. He cancels out even the normal order of inheriting bad mojo from the fruit of our choices. It's like the story of the prodigal son—God is waiting for us to return, and as a loving father, he is ready to fully allow us to inherit blessings instead of reap more bad consequences from the mistakes in our lives.

PERFECT LOVE CASTS OUT FEAR

One meeting I was at when I was young had a very loving prophet ministering. He called out one of my new close friends who was around ten years older than me. He had just got saved out of a life of drugs and sexual addiction and had had hundreds of female partners. He was scared to get tested for AIDS because he knew in his heart he was probably HIV positive. He felt like he deserved it after such an intense life of sexual destruction.

The prophetic man came up to him one-on-one, without knowing him, and said, "God wants to heal you of AIDS, or the threat of AIDS, and restore to you the life he intended you to have. Go get tested, and when you see that the result is negative, never be afraid again."

My friend broke down weeping, and I saw fear just melt from his heart about his life. A lie that he deserved HIV came out of his heart, and when he was tested, *he was negative.*

We Christians sometimes feel the need to see a natural type of justice occur, which would be the bad guy getting killed in our lifetime, or the thief getting caught and getting punished. It's like the American mentality that we deserve a happy ending. We begin to objectify humanity as God's enemies and objects of God's wrath.

Paul had to write to the Ephesians about this struggle we are also in: "For our struggle is not against flesh and blood, but against the rulers, against the authorities, against the powers of this dark world and against the spiritual forces of evil in the heavenly realms" (Ephesians 6:12 NIV). It is clearly defined as a war against corruption and powers and false authority. God never intended us to be at war with humanity. Jesus had to explain to some of his followers that he wasn't going to war or overthrowing the government because the kingdom he belonged to would bring full justice, not just temporary resolution.

We know that the world in its current state, without the help of Jesus, is dark. God doesn't have to add his power to crush what is already headed for destruction, but he *is* asking us to partner with redemption, transformation, and hope.

JUDGMENT PROPHECY

I am going to make a broad statement that will offend a few people: Most of the prophetic people who give words of judgment have been inaccurate. Very few can point out a prerecorded message from the event, but they'll try to claim the glory of it in hindsight: "I told my team about this one night," or, "I knew this would happen." A lot of the people who give judgment words have never taken the responsibility to track if they happen afterwards, so it's hard to build accountability and a track record or trust them. (We will go more into this later in the book.)

I have been around wonderful prophetic people who declare judgment, and then when others ask them why it didn't happen after the fact, they claim, "People must have prayed. . .", which implies two things:

1.   It was a word of warning, not a guaranteed occurrence, so they should prophesy it that way, if at all. There should never be a time when someone tells a region, city, or person that God will judge it/him without hope. God will allow the consequences of sin at times, and this is often misinterpreted as his judgment.

God is not in the business of bringing disaster or calamity directly to people who have made bad choices. It is obvious that the wages of sin is death and that when you make a bad choice you will reap at some point from it. God will, however (according to Scripture), protect his covenant with his people. He will move on behalf of the poor, the widow, and the orphan; and he will oppose people who violate children.

Sometimes Christians who prophesy earthquakes, tsunamis, droughts, and more are in actuality declaring that God (who loves and sent his Son to bridge the gap relationally) needs a reoccurrence of the price paid to make these things not happen anymore. In other words, "Because you, too, are separated in sin, you have no hope of redemption, so I have to destroy you. Jesus doesn't count for you because you rejected him too." That is a very sick gospel.

2. This prophecy was conditional and pointed out basically what people would reap based on their current sin, but informed them that they had a chance to repent and avoid those consequences. The conditions need to be defined and then tracked.

Number 2, is a huge one when people are declaring what God wants in their church, city, region, etc. They *have* to be accountable to defining the terms. God is in the business of speaking in ways we can understand so we can then change and transform from them. Is the prophet saying that because we have alcoholism over our region, God has to burn our crops by March 1 (a true story about an African prophet's prophecy that never happened)? If the word didn't happen, did that alcoholism rate change in a trackable way? If you can't track it, then it's not worth saying, because it makes God look like a crazy person. All negative prophecy should have a redemptive perspective or it's just not aligned with the nature of God.

Let's imagine you gave a word about a storm hitting because of sin, an earthquake happening because of corruption, etc., and the disaster occurred. If you can't define what has changed because of the word, then what is the word about in the first place? God doesn't just point things out; he loves the world and wants to transform people, not kill them off because he's mad at them.

WE ARE CALLED TO DISCERN BOTH GOOD AND BAD AND THEN BRING THE FATHER'S REPORT

As a Christian you are going to discern motives of people's hearts, bad politics, unhealthy patterns in education, terrible policy and procedure, greed, manipulation, and more, *but you are not bound to those circumstances.* Your opinion and perspective is also going to be influenced by the news media you watch, social media, popular opinion, and friendships—all of which will cause your discernment in certain things to be more acute (and possibly biased). We are called to discern the Father's heart, not just the black-and-white or the truth amongst lies. Sometimes seeing the truth without God's heart and perspective can bring destruction to the very relationships God wants to build. This can be very limiting and isolating, but when you can see through God's eyes, you are connected to love and can see the bigger picture. You are not bound to a cause; you are bound to love.

Let's say I can discern an acquaintance's struggle with lying about something that is not personal to me and I don't have much relationship with him. If I call it out just because I see it and know it can be dangerous, but I don't offer a process of healing or help for the person, have I just reinforced the shame behavior that causes lying or actually made him change?

THE TWO LIARS

Two of Jesus's friends were liars, and he didn't go directly after their weak character. He spent time with them building a culture of healthy relationship and good character. He even called things forth in them that he saw (based on his revelation from the Father) in the midst of their bad choices. At one point, Jesus called them both out on the fact that there was going to be or had been lying.

Jesus didn't call Judas out until almost three years into their relationship, and it was because Judas was at that point making terrible decisions that were hurting everyone around him—decisions that ultimately led to Jesus being handed over to be killed. It's amazing that even though Jesus could discern this, he didn't act on his discernment sooner (which is how most leaders lead today. They would have disqualified Judas and shut him out). Jesus, however, was making a kingdom, risk-filled investment in Judas, and he chose to treat him as more than his current choices. The culture of Jesus's heart acted as an incubator for both Peter and Judas.

Jesus told Peter that he would lie three times about him. He told him this out of mercy for Peter's weak character; he wanted Peter to know he still loved him, even after the fact. After Peter had denied his best friend, he probably thought obsessively about the fact that Jesus had known he would do it for a long time, but even at the Last Supper, Jesus chose to treat him as an intimate friend anyway. That reflection was probably Peter's only comfort. Jesus had been wonderful to him in the midst of pointing out his character flaw and prophesying his negative choice.

If the kingdom was just about principles of right and wrong, then Jesus would have never run after Peter after the resurrection and restored him through love. He would have judged Peter as unworthy and looked for someone more righteous. God isn't looking at our current weakness or lack of righteousness as a disqualifier, but he sees what we would be like if we followed him with our whole heart and loves us that way.

DISCERNMENT DOESN'T ALWAYS BUILD

We can see many US civil rights leaders just dwelling on the current truth of which human and civil rights are missing. They are not always seeing the big picture and looking beyond our current limitations the way some of the forefathers did, such as Martin Luther King Jr. He had prophetic vision and saw equality. He saw positions for men and women offered equally to every gender, every race, every country of origin, and every past. He had a dream that wasn't limited to the society of his day, and in just one generation, we have advanced significantly.

Those who aren't looking at what God has done and what we have voted in might only focus on what is not happening, and then fight for social justice and civil rights without the full perspective of what God has done and is doing. That is a dangerous way to approach issues, especially on a strong issue like social justice, because all justice starts with our acknowledgment that God has a plan. He plans to correct injustice through love, and he has already been working on it for thousands of years. I have met some incredible civil rights leaders who model this well, but there are also loud shouts from others that will not bring this nation forward because their declarations are not full of hope, love, resolution, change, or justice. It's the same in the church.

WE HAVE TO SEE WHAT GOD IS DOING, NOT JUST WHAT MAN IS NOT DOING OR WHAT THE DEVIL WANTS TO DO

When we begin to discern God's heart, not just the injustice, we live past our generation's eyes and see with God's vision. We see what God wants to do and we see who he *is* and what he *is* doing and we call our community into it. We have to call forth what is in God's heart as though it is fully available now, instead of looking at what's missing. That is why some Christians in the civil rights arena are negative and feel like we are going backwards. Some can see beauty in the fact that we have had our first black president—a direct fulfillment of Martin Luther King's dream. It's time to keep living the dream, not just fight for what we don't see happening.

We have to discern both good and evil but live in the good, the right, and the noble. We have to keep our eyes and affections fixed on God and see things from his heavenly perspective, living from the place of his presence and heart of love. We are often at war with his perspective, and the prophetic can either compound that war or bring hope. The Bible is often called the gospel of *good news!* Prophecy should reflect that.

GOING ONE STEP PAST DISCERNMENT

As I previously wrote, discernment is merely God's conversation starter. When you have empathy, compassion, passion, or a heart for justice, many of the things you discern will leave you feeling strongly emotional and spiritually sapped. You cannot stay at your starting point. God has given you discernment so you can pray and get *his* spiritual perspective. Sometimes God shows you what is not happening so you can define the void and pray a resolution from his heart. Sometimes he shows you what people are not doing so you can hear God's heart about what he wants to raise up. For everything you discern, there is a deeper, more original thought about it in God's heart.

In high school I went to a church that had a culture of discernment that hadn't matured into revelation, so people often would say, "That feels evil" about, say, a movie, without really knowing what it was about. I remember some of them boycotted *Robin Hood* with Kevin Costner because some of the women went and were desperately oppressed when the witch came on the scene. They came back with the report, "The movie glorified witchcraft!"

That was so out of context, because the witch and her demonic powers were not validated in the movie; the plot showed an evil that had to be overcome. Their "discernment" was pronounced as revelation that God didn't like the movie. Taken out of context, so many things could be inherently evil. Context is key to understanding heart and story. The Bible is full of evil characters looking really evil so that when you see them get torn down, you learn the nature of God. This is all context to good storytelling and gives us the ability to see real redemption.

Even worse, our young church would get what they called "checkmarks" or "checks" about different people's character or behavior. One time one of them had a "check" about my character (as a seventeen-year-old) and warned the pastor to be careful because of something they saw as potentially dangerous in my character. This was very destructive to relationship, because it offered problems rather than solutions through faith. It tore down the pastor's hope in me and put him in warning mode versus giving him the desire to see what God *was* doing in me and help keep me in grace. It took him over a year to trust me, but his lack of trust was not based on my behavior; it was based on a bad theological word. Years later he apologized to me for such an baseless lack of faith in my heart.

Discernment without going to the Father's heart can truly work like the worst witchcraft that any Christian can face. It's definitely a lot worse than seeing a witch in a movie. . . Any discernment outside of relationship can cause people to become political, manipulative, and divisive. We aren't called to discern *evil* as a goal; we are called to discern *God's heart*. That means sometimes we will see evil so we can see what God wants to do about it. If you take out the second step (listening for revelation), however, you can become as evil as the thing you discern without even knowing it.

I often tell people who are exceptionally discerning to fast from negativity for a while. In other words, spend six months ignoring your discernment, because your negativity is causing your focus to be off and your discernment has become critical instead of empowering. Just focus on what God *is* doing in every situation and ignore the enemy or humanity until you can stay in an attitude of victory in *who God is*. This scares people who rely on discernment and not relationship. They feel that if they don't discern, they'll be in danger of the world around them. Discernment was never supposed to be your main focus; relationship was.

CHAPTER 7

THE WAY GOD COMMUNICATES

THE YOUNG GROOM AND HIS BRIDE

I asked in a session recently, "Is there a Mary here with a son named Jonathan or John?" A young man raised his hand and said, "I am John and my mom is Mary." I was excited because it was such a specific word of knowledge, and I had more, but when I looked at him I saw a vision behind him. I saw heaven open up and there was a beautiful woman full of life and fire holding Jesus's hand. It was his wife, who I could tell had passed from this earth not long before. I began to cry because I was only married a few years at this point, and just knowing he had lost his wife was devastating to my new experience of marriage. I was grieving but also watching this beautiful picture unfold.

Jesus said to Jonathan, "Remember what Rachel told you in November? It was prophetic. Her heart is for you to have a full life, and she is so grateful that you and Mary took care of her while she was dying of cancer." I related this as a message to John, and he was shaken to the core.

He told me later that in November, his wife had told him she didn't think she was going to make it. She told him all the things she wanted him to do to be happy without her. She told him that his life would restart really fast after she passed away, and to not feel ashamed of moving on. It was a very significant talk, but he still felt guilty about moving on so quickly without her. A new job and some new developments (relationally) had happened fast, just like she'd said, and he wanted to honor the goodness of those things but was afraid to dishonor her. The word brought the resolution he needed. For me, it showed how complete God's love and desire for happiness is for each one of us. I hadn't really had an experience where someone from the cloud of witnesses was able to speak to Jesus and then have Jesus speak through me so clearly to someone she left behind, and it was beautiful, but it changed my paradigm.

BAD AND GOOD NEWS

Everyone in my life, including family and close friends, is always asking me how I hear God. I love that, because when we hear each other's experiences it can inspire the understanding of the mystery of God's voice. I have bad news that is actually really good news, and you already probably know it:

Prophecy is about relationship.

No two relationships are alike, and no one can teach you exactly how to be extremely intimate with God in the specific way you long for, but relational skills can be built. He has promised you his Holy Spirit to take you on this journey. I am learning about God by the way he communicates, even through my own gift of prophecy. Sometimes what he says to me is a stretch to my theology or understanding of psychology. Sometimes what I hear is so unusual that in hearing his message for someone else, I grow in my own choices to love and relate to his heart for me.

TEACHING YOU CREATIVE COMMUNICATION

I love that God communicates in so many ways. He first revealed himself in the Bible as a creator, and he is sooooo creative in how he does relationship with humankind. We get to understand his heart about these communications. He is a father first and a king second, not a king who is a father (meaning the father identity comes first). As his sons and daughters, he is more interested in communicating so that we do things *with* him rather than *for* him.

It would be so easy if God just gave us clear and direct words that we could obey, but mankind has proven over and over that we would rebel under any authority that isn't relationally driven. That's why God sent his Son to restore relationship. God's goal in talking to you is not to just be directive, corrective, or even direct. He wants to reveal his nature to you and rewire your brain with kingdom thinking and living. He wants to make your heart full and whole and help you to make the best decisions you can, not make them for you. That is why Jesus spoke in parables; he was changing the perspective of everyone around him to see from heaven's culture rather than earth's. He wanted to realign their heart attitudes and relational skillsets with those of heaven. One of my favorite passages in John is when the disciples had been listening to Jesus for a while and blurted out, "Now you are speaking clearly and without figures of speech. Now we can see that you know all things and that you do not even need to have anyone ask you questions. This makes us believe that you came from God" (John 16:29 NIV). When they said this, they thought Jesus had changed the way he talked, but in all reality, they had learned the culture of his heart and could understand his words from his perspective . . . after a little over three years of being with him.

We have a God who doesn't want to be listened to as a boss or leader. He wants to be known by his heart, personality, and Spirit. He created mankind for companionship, and many of the ways he speaks will be through parables, which is deliberate on his part, so that we have to seek his heart to know his mind. So many of the parables God gives us are in signs, pictures, and impressions. These are as foreign as tongues to us until we understand them, meaning they are for our spiritual benefit. The world around us may get nothing out of them until we have grown in what God is trying to tell us and share it.

SPEAKING AS A FATHER IS WAY DIFFERENT THAN AS A COMMANDER

I grew up in a relatively healthy family with a wonderful mother and father (thanks Larry and Stacia!). As I was growing up, my dad and mom would dream with me about what I wanted to be when I was grown. We went through all the normal phases a boy goes through: an astronaut, a fireman, a soldier, and then some unconventional ones for our family: an artist, an actor, a musician, etc. My parents didn't have an answer for me, but they wanted to parent me into finding my own dream and making powerful life decisions myself. What terrible parents they would be if they gave me no identity development but chose my career, school, wife, and city of residence. I would feel like life was contrived, and I certainly wouldn't really be living. But my parents helped me to dream. They formed character in me to the point that when I started making my own young-man choices, they got to enjoy healthy parental pride for what was going right. They were there for me when I made even some avoidable mistakes that were part of my self-discovery. In both processes, I felt enjoyed by them. They asked the hard questions so that I could find identity myself; they didn't control that process.

They would have hated having to direct all the choices, or have me rely on them to tell me what color shirt I should wear each morning, when they raised me to be a free, strong, powerful thinker. It would have pained them if I'd said to them, "I just want to be completely average," or, "I am going to go on welfare because I can't decide. I will let the government pay my way through a shutdown life."

Part of the Father's joy is in developing you and then watching you be strong and make great, very real choices. He enjoys seeing what his nature produces in you and what you create with it. He in no way created clones, slaves, or servants. He has always wanted partners who are free and powerful thinkers. We get caught up asking for healing gifts to heal diseases like cancer, which is noble, but when we come into full identity, we will encourage sons and daughters who want to be scientists and empower them with a creative heart and faith that believes they can cure cancer.

Some people want God to speak to them about everything because they have no identity. They don't believe in their ability to make good choices or to be empowered to be truly free. They can't make a life decision without saying, "God told me." In regards to my parents' methods, it would make my parents look bad and me extremely immature if I relied on their stewardship of my life as an adult. It actually sends a mixed message to the world: God loves me but he doesn't trust me to make good choices, so he directs everything I do.

"Gifts are free, but maturity is expensive." BILL JOHNSON

Because God wants us to have a strong identity, he talks through his nature more than he does through direct words. In this way, the more mature we get, the more we begin to rely on God's nature inside of us. We need less direct communication. We start to partner with God instead of just hope he will communicate as if we were still children. We no longer need to be told what is good and right for us because we have the deepest sense of who he has made us to be—both in our gifts and talents, and also in our personality, leadership style, relational style, etc. We have his Word, which we meditate on until it becomes our nature too. We protect the value of these things by making better and better choices, and when we fail, we lean into him—not so he will just make everything right, but so that we can allow him to walk us through them toward a deeper "knowing" of both his heart and ours. He works all things for the good of those who believe by helping our heart, character, and nature align with his along the way.

I love the current move of life coaching, because fathering should feel like developing life skills and empowering heart choices, not just creating boundaries. The more we grow in confidence to live *from* God's nature, the less we will even ask for directional words. They won't be our go-to anymore when we have to make decisions. We will always include God, but we will understand it is his joy to allow us to make powerful decisions. We will also be open to when he does intervene, because we know he is a good father. If he asks us to change geography, we'll know it's because he has something awesome for us somewhere else; it will be a place where we can develop more of his nature and be a blessing to those around us.

Lastly, think about it this way: If your daughter came to you at twenty-four and said, "Pick out my husband; I am afraid of my own choices," you would feel terrible as a parent. When she's in her mid-twenties, you are not trying to make her choices for her; you are trying to reaffirm her confidence, her identity, her ability, her leadership, her beauty. You are no longer directing her but walking *with* her. If she asked you this, it would actually hurt you. Part of you would understand that her asking you this was a direct result of your parenting gone wrong. It would be obvious she wasn't thinking right, and it's not right thinking in Christians.

If she made a great choice though, it would feel like your reward as a parent. Your glory is your children's goodness at work. God's glory is our manifesting his heart and character through our lives and choices.

GETTING HIS NATURE THROUGH SIGN OVERLOAD

For years God would chase me with the number 11:11. Every time I looked at a clock, it felt like it was 11:11. I would get an $11.11 receipt for coffees, or the tax on a meal would be $11.11. I would get put in hotel rooms with the number 111 or 1111 all the time. Then the number 22 started glaring at me as well. It was constant. Both of these numbers would appear even in people's prophecies for me, but I felt like they were all hints for a huge punchline I would understand someday. It got so ridiculous that for over fourteen years, both numbers appeared. I had a *lot* of revelation about them and about Scriptures they related to, but my understanding of their meaning still felt incomplete.

When I was moving to Los Angeles, I had a lot of hardships facing me. Two of my prophetic friends had decided Los Angeles wasn't going to exist very soon, that an earthquake would destroy it, and that I was in danger if I moved there (this was back in 2006-2007). Several supporters stopped supporting us, saying, "If you move virtually anywhere else we can support you, but LA is evil." Just a whole lot of human crap happened, but we pressed through because I had heard from God about moving to Los Angeles since I was sixteen. Now, twenty years later, it was time.

After being in LA for a year, I was in love with it. I knew I was right where I needed to be. During this time we saw 11:11 and 22:22, or variations of it, all the time. It was so apparent that the appearances of them started accelerating. It became haunting to us (more than Linda Blair was haunted in *The Exorcist*, but on the good side). During that time we also had the most criticism we ever had experienced from good friends outside of LA. They were in churches around the country, and they wanted to see transformation come to Los Angeles (but FYI, we had more support than critics).

So during this period, a Methodist pastor came to me from downtown LA. He said God had told him to bring me downtown and show me something. He didn't understand why, but he was trying to be obedient. He took me to one of the places he went to pray on Olvera Street in little Mexico (where there is a little square with the oldest church in LA on it. It's still open and still meets there, and it's where he was on staff.)

"There is a plaque here about the founding families of the city. It was put in by the city to commemorate something special, and you need to see it. By the way, this is the exact center of the city, according to Los Angeles County. This is where our city truly started."

We went to the plaque and I looked down, my toes standing a few inches from it, and began to cry. 11:11 and 22 came together, not just scripturally, but deep inside of me. It was done. I finally knew the reason I was getting them: The plaque read, *The City of Los Angeles was formed by 11 men, 11 women, and 22 children.* It took God twenty-one years to show me, through a parable, that he wanted to build a family culture in LA that he would export all over the world. Even in how the city was formed, there was a parable of his revival culture. Revival looks like family first, and here I was, receiving this message after all those years of being haunted by numbers.

God didn't want to just tell me, "Revival looks like family; go to LA and build one." He wanted my nature to change, my heart culture to be developed, my love to mature. He used revelation to intrigue me, and he kept it mysterious so that at every level of understanding, part of me would change. He also wanted me to be aware of his presence and heart each time I noticed those numbers. He wanted me to be aware that my love for Los Angeles was spiritual, not sentimental. He wanted to root in me a deep sense of connection to the LA that he was calling me to.

"God gets glory from concealing things; kings get glory from investigating things" (Proverbs 25:2 CJB).

Revelation is never a straight road. It is Dorothy's journey in *The Wizard of Oz*; it is Lucy's story in *The Lion, the Witch, and the Wardrobe*. It is a series of events that form his story in you that changes your DNA and aligns you with his. If you understand this, you will be a good steward of these ways God speaks. You will journal, you will remember, you will interpret, you will be patient.

REVELATION IS PROGRESSIVE

"God had to give me a revelation to understand the revelation, and that was after I already had a revelation!" JERAME NELSON

God never speaks just once. As a matter of fact, ask anyone who has ever heard the voice from heaven if they would mind if he never spoke again, and you will get a resounding *no!* God is eternal, and he starts sentences in the beginning of our lives that he finishes in later years. He is constantly weaving his prophetic message through circumstances and through our history. So much of life can be interpreted, just like the Jewish prophetic journey from the beginning into the book of Acts.

When we understand that revelation is not just direction or just a complete thought for the *now*, but that it is God sharing himself relationally with us for a bigger picture of connection, then we will talk to him and listen differently. Also, we will listen for his voice to create more connection with him, not to just solve current problems or get what we want or need. So much prayer is self-centered and can even be selfish—it's all about what we need for now with no forethought into developing our relationship with God, his heart, and his love for us. He wants to share with us every day and not just be around to fix something, but to walk with us.

CHAPTER 8

THE REVELATION GIFTS

I love the revelation gifts. I love them because they create context to go deeper with people. I love them because they bridge us to people we may not talk to on a deeper level. I love them because they are transformational. I love what they have done in my life.

When people use the term "prophetic ministry," they are most likely referring to the use of prophetic gifts. The Spirit of God is referred to several times in the Bible as the spirit of revelation. He is the revealer of relationship with God, God's will, God's intent. When we understand each of these tools and how they work, we can set clearer goals on how to participate with them. When you know the difference between a word of knowledge and a word of prophecy, it helps you to know how to direct the word, if it needs to be tracked, if you should ask a question or make a statement, etc. The more education, the clearer the gift can become.

THE GIFT OF A WORD OF WISDOM

Definition: Words of wisdom are a revelation on what to do with what is inside of us. Or it's revelation to interpret and give strategy to our spiritual perspective, or even to other personal prophetic words. Getting words of wisdom is like having a coach or counselor explain what is going on in your heart or about your spiritual or life journey. The word of wisdom is the supernatural revelation, by the Holy Spirit, of divine purpose or counsel from the mind and will of God.

One day I was brought in to do a prophetic prayer time with a man running for president in an Asian nation. He was a Christian every believer in the country seemed to have a strong opinion about (some good, some bad). Many of the Western ministers were invited to pray with him before the elections, and this was making many pastors and leaders, let alone business leaders and other candidates, nervous. When we walked into his office, he was very tired. I could tell running for president was the most difficult thing he had ever done, and I have no experience in politics, so I couldn't imagine what he needed or how I could be helpful. We prayed for a few minutes, and I knew he didn't need one more nice Christian encouragement. He needed wise spiritual counsel.

I began to pray and speak to him. As we sat together, I shared with him my discernment on some of his past words and spiritual perspectives, and shared a spiritual perspective about his campaign, his presidency, his heart, and his family. It was to give him wisdom on how to apply his faith to the words and how all the words were tied together, which formed a map for his faith. He seemed to feel very empowered. By the time I left, we felt very connected.

I got an e-mail the next day from his chief of staff thanking me. He said they had needed a counselor to help work through all the different spiritual and political perspectives, and they felt like they now knew how to go forward based on our time together. I was amused at the whole situation because I knew I didn't have the wisdom to pull that off, but through my relationship with the Holy Spirit, I was able to lend wisdom from heaven to this man who did end up becoming president.

I love when the Holy Spirit comes on you when you are praying or processing with a friend or associate and you feel like you are the best counselor, financial advisor, life coach, etc., and then it lifts and you realize it was part of God's prophetic Spirit, not your wisdom. I am always an amazing counselor and speaker when God shows up!

THE PROPHETIC—A NEW TESTAMENT EXAMPLE

Agabus gave the most amazing word of wisdom through a prophetic message to the early church (detailed in Acts 11). This wasn't a judgment word; it was about a weather phenomenon that was going to happen, and God wanted to grant grace to his people through clear direction. The disciples interpreted, through his message, that the word of wisdom on what to do was to store and send food to the brothers in the region with the famine. How amazing! Oh, that we would hear God like this for each other as nations!

Peter was given a word of wisdom after receiving his vision of unclean foods and the message that he was supposed to eat them. The Spirit told Peter to go to Caesarea and meet with Cornelius. It was a very clear word that led to Peter endorsing Paul's message that everyone was worthy of the price Jesus paid on the cross, not just the Jews (see Acts 11).

THE GIFT OF PROPHECY

Definition: Prophecy is the ability to know what is available or what is in the heart of God for the future. It is knowing what God wants to do or what he is developing someone or something to do. Prophecy makes people feel what it might feel like in heaven, as if they have some of the hope that is in eternity now. They can feel like the rest of their lives are important and worthy because they are eternal beings, and they matter to God *on the most consequential levels.*

Before I met my wife, she and two other friends came to a conference in Phoenix, Arizona, that I was speaking at. I had the opportunity to pray and prophecy over her and her friends. One of her friends, Lauren, had a semi-secret passion for makeup artistry. She had done her friends' weddings and special days, but she worked as a manager in a major corporation, and it was a great job.

I called her out, not knowing she loved makeup, and said, "You are creative, and you will only be truly happy when you follow your heart into a creative career. There is a calling of makeup artistry on your life so you can nurture people. You will do makeup artistry for the entertainment industry. God is going to give you a platform to their hearts through your craft."

Lauren had a moment better than *aha*. She had a God moment in which the secret desire of her heart was validated. It gave her courage to look past the good job and go for a great, but risky career in makeup, which was her true passion. She was able to leave the normal job that provided a lot of security and pursue her dream, and you know what? She is super successful at it and we love hearing her adventures. She needed to be seen for what God wanted to call her into, not just for what she was currently doing.

The gift of prophecy can be defined as the supernatural ability to speak the mind of God for the future by the inspiration of the Holy Spirit. Prophecy can include any and all of the revelatory gifts. Prophecy speaks to men for their encouragement, strengthening, and comfort (see 1 Corinthians 14:3). Prophecy may also convince (14:24), instruct (14:31), direct (Acts 13:2), and predict (Acts 27:10).

In 1 Corinthians 14:1, Paul commissioned us to love and then said to eagerly pursue spiritual gifts, especially prophecy. This word "prophecy" means to divine, to speak under inspiration of the Holy Spirit, to foretell the future. It's such a powerful statement. Why did Paul tell the Corinthians to go after this gift with full passion? It's because it connects people to two things:

1. It connects people to God's heart for their very precious lives here on earth. Jesus said he came to give us life and life abundantly. Prophecy connects a suffering world to the fact that there is a better day to be had. It reshapes their hope to believe God has bigger and better plans, and he works all things in our future to the good of those who love him.

2. It helps to connect humanity to eternity. Prophecy helps people believe not only in what God is saying for their lifetime, but also for their eternity. They come into alignment with the truth that they are eternal now and that they want to live forever. When you walk into good things God has prepared for you here on earth, it gets you divinely motivated about what he has prepared for you in heaven. Prophecy encourages heavenly perception because it makes you aware of the God who lives there, the One you get to spend all eternity with.

THE GIFT OF WORDS OF KNOWLEDGE

Definition: Concerns supernatural revelation by the Holy Spirit about a person's life. The information is not solely discerned, but includes specific facts that will help bring someone's heart closer to the mind of God. Words of knowledge help people feel known by God so they will believe more deeply in the truth. A word of knowledge usually comes right before a prophecy, healing, or miracle in order to bring faith for its release.

I was in Redding, California, at the Bethel Church Leaders Conference that they have twice annually. Pastor Bill Johnson had asked me to come up and minister prophetically. This wasn't the first time I had done this at a leaders' advance, but I was nervous because I had information, and I was waiting on the presence of God to connect his heart to my words.

Before the meeting, I had put a small list of words of knowledge with names, dates, and details into my phone. There was nothing but a bunch of facts on the screen, but I brought it prayerfully in hopes they would be connected to people who were there. I was super nervous, because words of knowledge on this level of faith were new to me, and the whole room would know if they were accurate right away. You can hide behind parables and not necessarily grow in accuracy very quickly, but a word of knowledge is instant.

I spoke over the microphone nervously, knowing that just about everyone in the room was a senior leader coming to experience more of God through Bethel, not more of my prophetic ministry. I was an unknown add-on, and most of the people were expecting Pastor Bill only, so if it wasn't good, it would be more of an interruption than an added blessing. I was aware of that and was pressing into God, taking the opportunity seriously but still trying not to be in performance mode. Pastors Bill and Beni Johnson and the team were so reassuring toward me that I was excited to just try.

"Does this make sense to someone? [made-up address] 320 Sycamore Lane?" I looked around the room and there was a pause. Then a booming voice said, "That is my home address, which is unlisted . . . ." It was Bishop Joseph Garlington of Covenant Church in Pittsburg. I didn't have any relationship with him, but I did know who he was. I was blown away that I knew his address, but there was more. "Do these numbers make any sense to you?" and I started listing an area code and the first four digits of a phone number, when he said, "Stop! That's my home number!" (LOL)

Now Bishop, who has had many prophetic words that have helped shape what he is doing and empowered his prophetic gift, was completely open at a core level to hear what God would say through me, a stranger. He knew God was revealing something to me after I received his unlisted home address and phone number, and it opened up his expectation. The beautiful word that followed would not have had the same impact if it hadn't opened with words of knowledge—words that made him feel targeted by the Spirit and brought him to a whole new level of faith.

ONE OF THE LEAST USED AND MOST IMPORTANT PARTS OF PROPHETIC MINISTRY

Words of knowledge have been a lost art in the prophetic arena, hardly focused on except when ministering healing. For some reason people haven't pursued words of knowledge as a goal for the prophetic for some time, but words can open a heart faster than a Rabbit corkscrew wine opener.

When people hear that God knows precious details of their lives, whether historical or current facts, it helps them to feel known by God and cared for by him. I can't tell you how many people have been considerably and instantly moved by God's love through words of knowledge I've given—both the richest of the world and the poorest. This impact of love should be a priority when pursing the prophetic gifts. Words of knowledge contain supernatural revelation (from the Holy Spirit) of specific facts that will help to bring someone's heart closer to the mind of God. One of my favorite recent stories about giving words of knowledge:

A man came to a meeting I was doing in an oil town in Canada. He came because he was concerned about his mother being affected by our conference. She had come home so inspired by the meetings so far that she had been advertising them to her family members and trying to get them to come. He was in his thirties, and he was worried our meetings were focused on finances or on cultish phenomena. As he watched me prophesy, he thought I must have had a good detective on my team. Then I pointed at him and asked, "Is your name Bob?"

"Yes," he said.

"Is your wife's name Camille?"

He said yes again. Then I went through all his children's names and their addresses. The whole time he looked at me as if this was completely normal. He was stoic because he thought I had somehow looked it up on the Internet, or I had a team member speaking to me.

I gave him a powerful prophetic word, but he was cold as ice. Then I heard the voice of the Holy Spirit say, *He doesn't believe you, so ask him one more thing. Ask him if he has a dog named Bandit.* I did, and this big man's man began to cry.

I had no idea why this man, this oil industry rigger, was crying now. You see, he didn't believe anything I'd said that could have been researched, but his family had lost its dog and he had just adopted a replacement dog the day before, and no one anywhere (including his mom or rest of his extended family) knew he had done it. This was a tender spot for him, so when I said the dog's name, he knew everything else I'd said was real and that I hadn't researched him. He encountered the love of the Father through the whole message.

MANY FACETS TO GOD'S VOICE

I would encourage you to read other prophetic books (by prophets like Graham Cooke, James Goll, Kris Valotton and others) that teach a step-by-step process on developing specific areas of the prophetic. There are more ways God speaks—dreams, dark sayings, parables, visions, impressions, etc.—and I encourage you to keep educating yourself so that all of these become tools in your belt, not scary subjects you can't touch or work with because you don't understand them.

CHAPTER 9

PROPHETIC POWER IS RELATIONAL POWER

I felt a heat on my ear as I took the stage. I was shaky inside, like I hadn't eaten or had drunk too much coffee. I could feel as though soda pop fizz was fizzling on the left side of my body on my skin. I also felt an emotional euphoria that was almost being projected into me. What a strange group of sensations!

"The worship leader who just led. I just heard a song by the singer Tiffany: 'I think we're alone now.' Is your wife's name Tiffany?" I asked nervously, but full of anticipation. I didn't know where this was going.

"Yes," he said, and held up Tiffany's hand, who was right next to him. "Does Clay Aiken have anything to do with you?" I asked, as in my heart and mind I saw flash of the face of the American singer.

"Yes, that is our last name, Aiken," he said.

I gave some more words to them that encouraged them, but then I saw two names and Missouri. "Is there a Chris and Laura? In Missouri? " I said. They were their cousins.

Then I went beyond a word of knowledge and prophetic ministry—I looked behind them and saw something much more real. I somehow saw into heaven, and a little boy was running with Jesus, holding hands with him. I instantly knew a bunch of information about the boy, as if it was downloaded into me like a computer downloads information, but this came with an abundance of love and connection to the little boy and his family.

I said out loud: "I see a little runner in heaven! He couldn't run on earth, but he is running in heaven. He is running, holding hands with Jesus, and praying over the destiny of the family!"

Mr. Aiken's cousins had just lost their little boy to Parkinson's a few weeks before. His dad was a runner, and he loved running so much that he actually named this boy Runner, so when I used this phrase that I didn't even mean to use, God was intentional through it.

The family needed heavenly resolution that only God could bring. It had been such a painful experience to lose him when he was so happy and had fought so hard and taught everyone so much. I could feel now that same sense of the presence of God, but it wasn't just energy around me, it was him—a present God—standing with us. He was there, he was giving me his relational heart, he was the power from which I spoke and the power that was healing this family.

So much more happened in that ministry time. It wasn't just encouragement; the anointing of the Holy Spirit came and the anointing wasn't an it, it was the Father manifesting as if he was there, in person, through me. I could feel what Jesus must have felt, possibly in as great a way, as I fellowshipped with the Father's heart over this family. It brought his word alive in me and challenged unbelief in us all.

THE ANOINTING IS A RELATIONSHIP WITH GOD, NOT JUST A CONNECTION TO HIS POWER

"His presence is not upon us to be commandeered or directed by us. Instead, we are tools in his hand. If there is a dove resting on my shoulder in the natural (and I love that phrase 'and remained') and I don't want it to fly away, how am I going to walk around this room? Every step will be with the dove in mind. Every movement I make will be to preserve what I value most." BILL JOHNSON, MANIFESTO FOR A NORMAL CHRISTIAN LIFE

God longs to give us the power of his nature. He promised us his anointing. This is not just an electrical, metaphysical energy that will come on us; it is a person, the Holy Spirit who dwells in us and speaks to us from a source—the Father in heaven.

In modern times, the power of God portrayed by the church has not usually been displayed in its relational context, unlike the original Hebrew understanding of it. The whole Hebrew mindset is nothing like the Western or Greek mindset that much of our philosophy (in at least the Western church) comes from. The Hebrew mindset dictates that the power of God is his very nature manifested through his presence or connection to us. It's not a livewire of current or spiritual electricity; it's his love nature and the manifestation of his personhood.

Even in the New Testament, this different mindset is seen in Paul's description of God's anointing. He felt it so strongly that it affected him physically and emotionally. We see this when he says he is like a woman in the pains of childbirth that Christ be formed in them (see Galatians 4:19). That is not a picture of just getting whacked by energy or an ecstatic experience; it is a whole, beautiful, relational picture. Paul loved the Galatians as much as a woman having contractions who is about to birth her baby. The love of God is flooding through Paul's desire to see the nature of God formed in his people.

This relational nature cannot be separated from "the anointing" or "God's power" or "the gift." There has been a higher focus on character reformation than on anointing or power, but people don't just violate character when they sin; they violate relationship. The anointing is one's ability to connect to the nature of God through a very real and tangible relationship. (This might bring about spiritual manifestations, but the manifestations are not the goal of these experiences.) We need to love this connection more than anything, because when you care about keeping this connection to the Holy Spirit, you will say no to anything violating it. We must focus more on our relationship with God's heart than on our character, because the source of character reformation is his love.

> "Holy Spirit is not an IT, but a HE. He is a person and HE wants you to know him, and when you know him, you will know God." JILL AUSTIN

John says we have an anointing that teaches and leads us into intimacy with Christ (see 1 John 2:20-27). We don't need anyone else to teach us this love, just like a woman doesn't have to be taught how to love her baby. We may need help growing in the skills it takes to steward this love, and we need a community to express and deepen this love, but it becomes second nature to grow into this love when living a life focused on God.

Our ability to manifest spiritual fruit in the prophetic depends on our union to the Holy Spirit, not our gifts or skill level. Real gifting that builds the kingdom comes from deep love. There will be a great distinction in the days ahead between inspired gifts (gifts that come from this abiding or resting intimacy with the Holy Spirit) and gifts or skills that operate just by the grace of how we were designed. This is why Paul said God's gifts and his call are irrevocable (see Romans 11:29). We will always have the tools that God designed us to use, but whether these tools are connected to his power and nature or just the power of humanity is up to us.

Sometimes even church people have no identity in God, but they still can be gifted, and this has been so confusing historically. How can a singer write such an amazing song that my faith connects so deeply to, but then that same singer falls into a terrible disconnect with his relationship with God, or we find out later had none at all? Wasn't his song glorious? Wasn't his skill amazing? Weren't the words full of beauty? He was made to sing, and God has given all of humanity access to its full, uniquely designed, eternal toolset, but we can't minister these gifts full of heaven's worth, life, and fulfillment without relationship with the Father.

My parents taught me that to be holy meant to love your relationship with God and protect it at all costs. I watched my dad model purity in regards to women because he was protecting his relationship and sexuality with my mother. He wasn't just saying "I will be pure!" as a statement of trying to be right and not wrong. He was protecting my mother by staying pure because he had so much invested in his marriage and our family. She was so worth the protection. The moment he breaks that purity, he breaks the connection that he values most, so it's easier to walk in purity when it is relationally motivated.

> "Developing a life in God's presence above all else is the only way to fulfill our God-given destinies. Keys to our callings are released when we spend time there." HEIDI BAKER

WILL YOU CHOOSE RIGHT OR WRONG OR LOVE?

Adam and Eve chose a tree, which in essence was choosing knowledge over relationship. They broke their connection to God and violated the purity of their relationship to heaven by making a different choice. To live a successful Christian life, we have to choose to receive purity and anointing through our relational connection to God. If we love God with all of our heart, mind, and strength, then we will spend all of our time letting his love, Word, and presence build our character in order to protect and advance the relationship. If we are not love motivated but rule motivated, we can build character around a ministry or gift—for a time—but we risk not being able to maintain it with the same passion. Following rules is an intellectual choice that our hearts may or may not follow, especially when obedience is often dependent on circumstances.

To love the anointing is to love the intimacy we have with God—the source of all the power to change and be eternal. To love character, gifting, ministry, or occupation first will eventually bring us to a place where we violate this relationship for the sake of building influence or impact. We must make little adjustments in ourselves every day to keep pursuing God and to keep him first. Then his power will flow through us, because it is relational power before it is governing power or educational power.

PROPHETIC POWER STARTS WITH LEARNING HOW TO BE AN ENCOURAGER, BUT IT DOESN'T STAY THERE

A prophetic attitude is birthed by people looking to bless what God is doing on the earth. People who grow in the prophetic the quickest are the people who are already naturally encouraging everyone around them.

I love my wife because she is always complimenting people out of a genuine place of affection. Whether it's my wife telling the crazy fro hair girl that her hair is the most amazing she has ever seen (she secretly wants a fro), or her friends that they look radiant, my wife is a constant vault of words of affirmation. It opens people's hearts, and they're happy to be around her because they feel valued. Words of encouragement don't come as naturally to me. It's not a strength of mine and not one of the primary ways I receive love, so I have had to put time into practicing and developing this skill. Yes, that's right, Shawn Bolz is not a natural encourager . . . and yet I prophesy encouraging things over dozens of people a week. That should give some of you faith (if you lack that love language or desire it to come naturally). It is so worth the developmental process, because it's a skill that every relationship not only needs, but requires.

This is how a healthy prophetic attitude starts—we get used to building people around us. We get accustomed to being encouragers. Where it gets powerful, though, is not in the complimenting of people's nice white teeth. The power of God manifests when we take on the attitude of Paul (that I mentioned in an earlier chapter). "Do you know how I feel right now, and will feel until Christ's life becomes visible in your lives? Like a mother in the pain of childbirth" (Colossians 4:19).

Something begins to inspire you when you see the world around you through God's heart for it.

Paul describes his vision of what the Colossians would be like if they were fully formed in Christ. It's an attitude that can only be born from fellowshipping with God's heart to *see* the people around you. You start to feel as though the gap between God's heavenly heart and his people is closing. Your very life becomes a bridge over that gap. Your faith and love stretch from God's own desire to your sphere of influence. I love how passionate Paul was in describing this! He was in the pains of labor, like a mother, praying and believing that this revelation of Christ would be fully formed in them. If you want prophetic power, a part of you will begin to adopt and love the world around you—which is the original vision of the Father.

God knew what he was doing from the very beginning, and he shapes the lives of those who love him as he shaped the Son's life. The Son stands first in the line of humanity he restored in his original and intended shape, and we stand with him there—fully atoned for, fully restored to our original design, fully alive in the Father's heart of love. After God made the decision about what his children should be like, he followed it up by calling people by name. After he called them by name, he set them on a solid basis with himself. And then, after getting them established, he stayed with them to the end, gloriously completing what he had begun (see Romans 8:29-30).

Paul, as he looked at Jesus, understood what restored humanity looked like. God's original, intended desire had never been demonstrated until Jesus showed up, but seeing Jesus helped Paul see the goal for all of humanity.

When we settle for a lessor vision, like upgraded humanity, we will not have the prophetic power we seek because we will have placed a cap on how far someone can grow in God.

SOUTH KOREA

Consider South Korea: In just one generation it has gone from a developing country to a fully developed country. It has industries that compete with the most developed in the world. Historically, Korea has been one of the most occupied countries in the world (by other nations). Koreans are not a warring people, but they are very industrious, entrepreneurial, and gifted. Throughout history, enemies tried to take advantage of their country, their people, and their resources.

Back around the time of the Korean War, a group of Christians in Canada were praying about how to help Korea. They saw in their hearts a developed South Korea and asked God for a strategy to bring that about. He showed them that if they rallied Westerners to finance one child each through education, then this education would become a foundation for the future greatness of the country. They used this prophetic word to start one of the greatest humanitarian organizations for children in history: Compassion International. (How many readers, I wonder, have supported a child by sending money to a Compassion International child sponsorship project.) The first generation of Compassion International kids that graduated college had a knack for building, and they helped lay Korea's foundation in government (one was even one of the first Supreme Court justices), education (many became teachers right away), religion (many became Christian pastors and leaders), and industry (many started businesses). It was such a pivotal movement that it is still referred to by many of the South Korean government leaders I have met. South Korea began its greater development into what it is today because God invested a vision of its future to Christians, organizations, and other groups. He gave them the faith to help Korea become what it is today.

Prophetic power comes when we see God's original design over nations, cities, people groups, industries, children, etc. What would Congo look like fully developed, and who has the courage to ask God to show what he wants to do in that nation, one of the most mineral rich nations of the world? This is how prophetic power comes. You can't listen to the war report, the popular report, the opinion papers, the religious report. You have to hear God's heart report—HIS *original* plan and design and HIS *current* plan of action. It will go against everything you have seen and heard. It's easy to hear reports about what is not happening in the nations, but you can flip it around and speak of what *can* happen. Even the United Nations will change dramatically when we start to help steer these reports over nations to be seen through a heavenly lens. We want to listen to God's heart instead of the critical mass.

RELATIONAL POWER COMES FROM CONNECTION, NOT CONVERSATION

Christians oftentimes come across as experts on any subject, even if they are not educated or connected to the subject. We feel a responsibility to really pastor the world into relationship with God and risk being out of control more than we risk being in love. To have true power in relationship to those around us, we have to understand emotional intelligence and practice self-awareness. The more mature we get in love, the more we depend on prayer and our connection with people versus our conversations with them.

When my parents cook, after fifty years of marriage, they barely talk. They have had so many conversations, they now relate through uncommunicated conversation. They can cook a whole meal and navigate around each other without any effort. God's nature is like this through us. He doesn't need our words; he needs our hearts first. Sometimes through seeing someone, our prayers and our choice to stand with *who he is* is more connecting than to communicate something to him. Sometimes when God gives us revelation, it builds an authority in our hearts to love individuals. As they overcome something that we were praying for them for, it helps us to live in an attitude of celebration. Even before it's a verbal thing, the love for them lives deeply in our hearts.

"There are times in the prophetic ministry when words we receive for others must stay in the throne room...they are more powerful when converted into crafted prayer and spoken to the Father than when put into prophetic language and ministered to human beings." GRAHAM COOKE, CRAFTED PRAYER: THE JOY OF ALWAYS GETTING YOUR PRAYERS

CHAPTER 10

REVELATION—EVERYONE GETS TO PARTICIPATE

God is so invested in his love for humanity that his love can be seen everywhere. Not only that, he is constantly pointing it out to everyone, trying to make the connection with all of humanity. He is giving us every chance we can have at the life he intended us to have. The presence of God is on the whole earth.

"'Am I a God who is near,' declares the LORD, 'and not a God far off? Can a man hide himself in hiding places so I do not see him?' declares the LORD. 'Do I not fill the heavens and the earth?' declares the LORD" (Jeremiah 23:23-24 NASB). "And one called out to another and said, 'Holy, Holy, Holy, is the LORD of hosts, the whole earth is full of his glory'" (Isaiah 6:3 NASB). There are so many Scriptures about God's glory covering the earth or covering humanity. This word *glory* is referring to his manifest nature. It's not a power, a thing, or just his governmental principles; it is our God! He is so big and has so much love that his love is everywhere. We know that if he is everywhere, this loving God is constantly trying to speak and connect to humanity.

Daniel had no problem with this concept. He even said God was the giver of a dream to a pagan king who worshipped false gods. Nebuchadnezzar was not a good man (he was probably more like Saddam Hussein, Stalin, or worse). He was no hero or fairytale king. Consider the fact that he made an image of himself and wanted everyone to worship it or die, and he almost killed Daniel and his friends over it. Yet Daniel still trusted in God's ability to speak to this king. That is miraculous faith, the kind that contemporary churches do not often have for the world around us.

We somehow have the narcissistic idea in the church that we are the voice of God, that we are the source for people to hear God, and if we don't speak, he will never be heard. God himself is the one who is speaking through creation, through people, through seasons, through industries, through Hollywood, and more. Many times he speaks through sources a Christian would have run from (in love).

Daniel, though, interpreted Nebuchadnezzar's mysterious dream and completely believed it had come from God's heart. He didn't fake it in an evangelistic attempt to sway Nebuchadnezzar, and he wasn't just doing his job. He had a deep love and respect for Nebuchadnezzar and Babylon, even though his people were exiles there. He modeled a type of love, honor, and service to a pagan empire that would be controversial today. Most Christians now are trying to get the world to agree with their arguments and don't even think the world has the ability to connect with God until they show up. God is bigger than us, and although he uses the church and his people as his main vehicles, he is not limited to us. God not only used Israelites in the Old Testament to speak to the world around them, he also used the world around them to save Israel and help Israel. This shows that God will move on his own behalf and love outside of our box.

Probably most Christians who visited a New Age fair today wouldn't expect God to actually be speaking to anyone there. We might judge New Agers as a group with mental illnesses, occult powers, demonic connections, or brilliant imaginations. Yet Daniel, in his day, believed that even in a pagan empire, God still wanted to speak. He had this level of faith because of his level of connection to God. He wasn't concerned with Nebuchadnezzar's other spiritual pursuits; he came knowing God's pursuit of Nebuchadnezzar was bigger. I want a faith like this!

JOSEPH

Joseph was really good at interpreting God's heart through dreams over Gentiles because he knew that God loved humanity. The dream God had given him when he was young wasn't just Israel-centric; it was a picture of the whole known world coming to be touched by God's authority through him. He wasn't looking at what he was doing as simple interpretations of human or demonic dreams; he knew he was interpreting the heart of the God of all the universe. He was revealing that heart to those around him so they could be connected to the God who is living and active and loving.

Pharaoh was impressed by the wisdom and revelation that came out of Joseph, and it caused him to create a bond of relationship with Joseph. Joseph helped define leadership to Pharaoh, who was already the most powerful man in his generation. Pharaoh was no Hebrew, nor have we ever read that he was converted. Although we know that Egypt was blessed, and that Pharaoh at least embraced some kingdom principles during his reign, he never forsook his gods, idols, or traditions. Our hope is that he did.

Even in Esther's case, God wasn't limited to someone's conversion to use her. King Xerxes never adopted Jewish customs or religion, but Esther's role in his life allowed for Israel's freedom from oppression, and it came to its restored place of prominence that God had promised.

Of course we desire that people around us come into full relationship with God, but God is not limited when people are not in relationship to him. He can be seen in the midst of all religious freedom as a marvelous light, and Christianity never dims because other freedoms grow. It just gets better and brighter.

GOD IS SPEAKING ALL AROUND US

We need to understand that God is speaking all around us. I think of the story I mentioned earlier about Peter going to Cornelius's house because God spoke to him. But God also spoke to Cornelius about his life, and Cornelius needed to meet with Peter to come into a full revelation of his spiritual pursuit. Isn't that amazing? God didn't just speak to Peter; he spoke to this Gentile in a way that caused Peter to have to change his theology to include sharing the gospel with the Gentiles.

Many of us also need to realize we will have a change in our belief system. We will start to acknowledge God's conversation that is already taking place all around us. For God so loved the whole *world!*

STORY OF A HAWAIIAN GIRL

I was in Hawaii in 2012. The condo I stayed at was beautiful, but its entrance was very close to the area's late night red light district. It was one block away from the main strip of Honolulu. I was hungry, and the only thing that was open after 10:30 when I got dropped off was a sub sandwich shop, so I headed there. It was a safe but seedy area after 10 p.m.

On the way, a Hawaiian in his young twenties tapped my arm and said, "Hey brah, you need anything tonight?"

I knew whatever he was selling wasn't anything I was buying, so I said, "Nope, I am good, just out for a sandwich."

"Come on, brah, you want some weed?" He put his hands to his mouth as if he was smoking some.

"No, that would make me hungrier. I just want a sandwich."

He laughed and said, "You want a girl?" and he pointed at three teenagers sitting on a closed diners' entrance that I hadn't noticed previously. It was two boys and a girl, all under eighteen, and the girl was only around fifteen. I got mad right away that he was trying to offer me this young girl, who was not dressed to be a prostitute like the others down the street. She looked very new or uninitiated in prostitution, but he was still offering her to me.

I said, "No, but I want to talk to her real fast," and walked over to her.

"Hey, I'm Shawn, what's your name?"

Her wannabe pimp came over and stood beside me, and seemed at ease with me talking to her based on our previous rapport.

"Kayla," she said, only slightly interested.

"What's your dream in life?" I asked.

"What do you mean? I don't have a dream," she responded.

"Well, I am a Christian and a pastor, and God talks to me about his dreams for me and helps me to form my own, so let's pray for a minute and ask God to show you a dream for your life. He thought of you for millions of years before he ever created you, so let's ask him what he thought about."

"Um, okay," she said, sort of confused but amused.

"Okay, borrow my faith and repeat after me, then wait for an answer. He is going to talk inside of you. Jesus, you love me and created me to enjoy life and live it to its fullness. Show me something that I was created for."

She repeated it and then said, "Whew!" and the two guys on either side were giggling until she said that. She looked like she legitimately felt she heard something.

"What did you hear?" I asked.

"I heard I should be a cook. . ." She said it with no insecurity, but had a look of wonder on her face like she had never expected that there could be anything else than the nothingness that had driven her to the streets.

"You mean like a chef? Do you like to cook food?" I asked.

"I think so . . . I haven't really done it much but yeah, I do!" She was amazed.

Before I let her ponder too much, I said, "God wouldn't give you such a great idea without giving you steps to take, like tomorrow, toward this dream, so let's ask him for some steps. Repeat after me: Father, you showed me something that I can do that would make me feel fulfilled and feel your heart. What is a step I can take this week toward it?"

She repeated that and then said, "Whoa!"

Her friend next to her had huge wide eyes and said, "What, Kayla?"

"God said to call my uncle who owns a diner! I never talk to him because my mom hated him and never let us call him or see him."

Notice, the first time she just heard something inside. The second time she knew it was God and acknowledged him.

"Kayla, do you promise me you will call him tomorrow and talk to him about this?" I asked. She promised she would. We were exchanging phone numbers when the guy next to her said he wanted a dream too, so we prayed and he had a similar encounter.

Kayla called me the day she talked to her uncle. He and his wife were Christians and had been praying for her, especially since she had run away. They were so happy that she called. She told them what God showed her. They hired her and brought her to live with them. She was an incredible asset to their business, such a hard worker, and very smart about ideas that could bring in a fresh crowd to the diner they owned (that was frequented mostly by older locals). The business grew fast as she partnered with them both on food and business topics.

It was so amazing, because when she was turning seventeen, she called me to update me on her amazing turnaround in life. She had been saved for a while, was living with her uncle and aunt, and had finished school early with a full high school degree. She managed their diner too. Then she said, "Uncle wants to open up another location and wants me to be a co-owner and help!"

I was excited for her. "Are you going to go to school for business or for culinary arts?"

"I don't have time. We are opening it next month! I will own it in just a few years! God's dream for me is bigger than I thought!"

I was so excited for her! Can you imagine? God spoke to her. I didn't prophesy to her. I simply helped her believe that God loved her enough to have a conversation with her.

He is such a personal God that he knows we won't always believe words someone else gives us, so he speaks to us. Pharaoh would never have met Joseph if Joseph hadn't had the dream and the interpretation of it, but God put the dream in Pharaoh's heart. Even if he had met Joseph, he wouldn't have believed the prophetic experience.

God is speaking all over the place. We hear him in the dumps in third world nations; we hear him at the nicest, billionaire-filled resorts in the world. God is not withholding his voice, but he is looking for people he can trust, friends he knows will love those he is speaking to in order to create the connection he intended with the revelation given.

Our good friend Cindy McGill is a master dream interpreter who goes out with teams on the streets all the time to interpret dreams. Sometimes she just asks people if they ever have a recurring dream, and almost everyone she asks says yes. Then, after they tell her what the dream is, she is able to speak into it. She reveals what God is saying through it and brings them resolution. Sometimes her revelations help them know it came from a God who loves them, and that he had something on his heart for them. People light up when they feel that nearness of God.

We have been presumptuous thinking we have to have, or be, the encounter for the world. The whole world is filled with God encounters; we just need to recognize them and position people toward a relationship with God so they can live in his abiding presence through salvation in Jesus.

IN THE HOTEL WITH THE ROOM-SERVICE GUY

I got to my San Francisco hotel room late from the meeting I had spoken at, and was very happy to get the last call they accepted for room service (thank God). My wife and I started talking on the phone, and we were in the middle of an engaging conversation while I got ready for bed when room service knocked on the door. I stayed on the phone with my wife, but when I opened the door, I noticed the young man who had my meal. Maybe it was because he was in street clothes instead of a uniform, but I also noticed he looked very down, and not just a little, and his face was white. He delivered the food and left in a hurry, but I immediately cared about him while knowing I would probably never see him again. I prayed for him quickly and reengaged with my wife.

After a few minutes, a knock came at the door again. It was him.

"Honey, I will call you back," I said and opened the door.

"Sir, I forgot to have you sign the bill."

"Hey, are you okay?" I asked, not expecting much back.

"I'd rather not talk about it."

"Okay, but if you do want to talk, I am a minister and might be able to help you. You feel kind of heavy."

God opened his heart to vulnerability. "Well, okay. My girl-friend just broke up with me." He had tears in his eyes but refused to cry.

I said, "Let's talk about this," and we both sat down. He told me his name was James and that I was his last run on a job he never takes in the hotel, but he had to fill in for their service staff. He then told me all about the relationship and how hard it was to be broken up with.

"She dumped me so fast. She doesn't even want to talk about it."

I wanted God to talk about it. "I am a Christian, and I believe God made us for relationships and he loves them a lot. He thought of you for eons before he ever created you, so let's ask him what he thinks about the relationship. I am going to ask him questions and you ask him for answers, okay?"

"Um, I don't believe in God and I'm not religious."

"Well, it won't hurt to try. Let's just do it this once then." I smiled encouragingly and closed my eyes. When I peeked, he was closing his too. "God, you made my new friend here, James, to thrive in relationship, so can you show him if this is the right relationship for this stage in his life?"

Before I even told him to ask God, he said, "It's not! I know she isn't right for me. I can feel it!"

"Did God show you that or you just know?" I asked.

"Both!" he said. He was a quick learner, and we were both in shock at how fast he heard.

"Let's ask him what he does have for you. Jesus, what do you want to show James right now about what you love about him? What about his life and relationships?"

"I'm supposed to do music!" he exclaimed, as if he had known it all along but just discovered it.

I wasn't expecting that. We were mostly asking about relationships. "That's amazing. Do you play an instrument? What did you hear?"

"Yeah, I am a musician, or . . . I was in high school. I won all kinds of awards, but my dad told me not to pursue it in college because music was a dead end for him and he was so disappointed that he didn't want me to go through that. I enrolled in a hospitality program in college and am interning here. I hate it! Just like I didn't like my relationship with my girlfriend, but it felt like the right thing to do."

"You need to stop doing the right thing and start doing what is real to your heart!" I let this sink in. "Let's ask God another question, because he obviously likes answering you. Let's ask him to reveal to you a step you can take toward following music."

We prayed for a little bit and he said, "I feel like I am supposed to go to the music conservatory in Los Angeles."

"That's where I live!" I told him.

He was excited. I was the first person he had met from LA in a long time. He told me about the program. We prayed he would have the courage to switch majors and that his parents would understand. At the very end he said, "I have never been to church. Is Christianity the one with the cross?"

I started laughing pretty hard, because the God of the cross just set him up for love and life, and he hadn't even demanded anything in return. I told James all about Jesus and his love, and James wanted to invite him into his life. That night, after God had already fathered him, touched his emotions and heart, given him courage, and caused him to laugh, James got saved.

RECOGNIZING GOD IN THE NORMAL

"Call to me and I will answer you. I'll tell you marvelous and wondrous things that you could never figure out on your own" (Jeremiah 33:3).

God wants to be present in a manifest way in our normal day. It is one of God's biggest gifts to us to manifest his presence in the here and now. We just need to learn how to invite him in or how to recognize when he is already there. We have to start believing that God is going to show up even when we aren't in the optimal frame of mind or mood. When you are a Christian, God is not dependent on you being in the right frame of mind to talk to people around you. You have asked God to come into your life, partner with you, and work through you. You have agreed that God can do whatever *he* wants through you. That means that even on the most normal, mundane days, he can be an awesome God in the midst of normality.

ON THE PLANE WITH A STUNT WOMAN

I was leaving out of California on a five-hour flight. I was up-graded and no one was next to me, which was glorious, because I was so tired I just wanted to sleep the whole way. At the last minute, right as the door was closing, a woman sat next to me. She looked devastated, and I remember in my normal humanness I whispered to God, "Please, God, let me just sleep." That was a normal human reaction to my overtiredness and my heavy workload that week. But deeper down in my core was that radical cry, "You can do any-thing, anywhere, anytime." God remembered that prayer and de-cided to cash in on it (gosh darn it).

We did a good job of ignoring each other until the flight atten-dant came over to ask us what we would like to drink. The woman said in response, "I would like the heaviest alcohol you have so I can just knock out and forget this ride ever happened."

Obviously, she had just gone through something that was crushing her emotions. I was worried, but also trying to be dis-interested, until she said that. I joked around and said, "I want to crash out too, but I will take water."

She looked at me and smiled. "Hi, I am Lisa."

"I'm Shawn."

"Well, Shawn, I work in the stunt industry in Hollywood. What do you do? I don't want to think about my life, so how about we focus on yours?" She smiled a genuine smile.

I really didn't want to talk, so I told her a version of what I did that probably wouldn't appeal to someone who doesn't know me or believe in God the way I do. I know, I know, right? Terrible of me to do. "Well, Lisa, I travel around the world as a Christian minister and teach people how to hear from God."

"That is so fascinating! I don't even really believe in God, so to believe you can hear from him must be wild! Can you tell me what you teach?"

I laughed out loud, knowing I wasn't going to get out of this God setup. Here was a woman whose emotions were heavy, who needed a distraction, and who was sitting next to me and wanted training on the prophetic. "Sure, Lisa," and I gave her a non-watered down course of not only prophecy, but also a lot of what I am writing here (God loves us and speaks to us).

She was so impacted that after a few hours of questions back and forth, she made a powerful statement. "You know what you need to do?" And she gave me a great version of every prophetic word that was dear to me tied together like a blueprint. It involved the entertainment industry, justice issues, and all kinds of stuff we hadn't talked about.

After she shared it all I had a question for her: "Lisa, you know what you just did, right?"

She looked stunned and gripped her chair. "Damn it!"

We sat there for a minute as she let it sink in.

"I just prophesied!" she exclaimed. The God she didn't believe in had just used her to speak to me because she had opened her heart.

She went on to tell me that the tragedy that had just happened was about an estranged family member she was in conflict with. He had just died, and she was feeling the pain and devastation of no resolution when she went to the funeral. We prayed together and she came to know God's love that day—not through me giving her an encounter or prophecy, but through hearing God herself. She ministered his heart to me and it wrecked her forever.

GOD IS SPEAKING TO EVERYONE WHO WANTS TO LISTEN, BUT HE ONLY HAS ONGOING, LONG-TERM CONVERSATIONS WITH HIS FRIENDS

Prophetic gifts are inherent to humanity. God has never stopped interacting with man in his supernatural way. We have many historical accounts of his doing so, and we can speak with him too—through prophecy. But if we don't understand that God is sovereign and speaks all the time, with or without us, we won't understand how big his mercy is. Or worse, we will create the idea that the world needs *us*, when really the world needs Jesus. I have seen so many prophetic people enter into elitism. They think that if they don't share *their* encounters or give *their* prophetic words, God won't move. It's a weird and hard thing to watch people go through, because it separates them from having and sharing the very relationship God wants to build. God wants to connect everyone to his heart through every means at his disposal, not have a few people who know the mysteries while everyone else looks to them, hoping for a glimpse.

The beauty of the prophetic is that it makes common the deep things of God. It doesn't withhold information. Most cults build their strength by knowledge brokering, or by a few holding the powerful secrets over the many. In Christianity, God has freely spoken the most precious secrets to people who don't even believe in him, because our power is in relationship, not knowledge or secret agendas. He uses the least of these to help encourage the masses, and he is not into elitism. He reveals his secrets to humanity because he treats us all as friends.

CHAPTER 11

ACCOUNTABILITY, A NEW WAY TO GROW

People everywhere now have a much lower expectation of prophetic gifts, mostly due to the severe lack of accountability over self-proclaimed prophets. If I told you stories of what people were willing to believe (through several dysfunctional ministries), you would be very sad, might possibly laugh, and then get sad again. Worse yet, many a reader could tell me even more horrible stories.

I think that when a lot of the prophetic ministries were birthed, especially in the 1980s-1990s, people were very excited about hearing God's voice. They were so busy equipping and training others to have faith for God to speak that there was very little time to give to the process of accountability. So much happened so fast. I think everyone was in reaction or survival mode. They were scrambling to learn how to steward God's voice and the promises that came with it. They were trying to figure out why God was speaking through such eccentric people—who seemed to be the chosen ones of that move. No one was thinking about what God wanted to do— to bring prophecy to the whole church for every believer—because in the movement, they didn't even know if it was going to last.

That was such a wild move of God. It was the first time in history that mass numbers of churches began to believe God wanted to speak to us about our normal lives and about the world around us. God wanted to converse with us about his heart—not just show it to us in the Scriptures, but bring the Scriptures alive through his Spirit! There were messages that dominated those times, like, "This is the season of the Word and the Spirit." At the same time, there was a lot of brokenness in the leaders stewarding these ministries. The only way they were addressing the inefficiencies was to teach on having more character than anointing or gifting. While this was helpful, it felt reactionary in many circles of Christians. It was not necessarily empowering, and sometimes even took away the hunger for prophetic ministry because of the damage people were creating. On one hand, people were witnessing the most amazing power demonstrations of God on almost biblical scales. On the other hand, some of those people, who were empowered for a minute and awed the world, fell into lives of depression, sexual indiscretion, money embezzlement, Christian cult leadership, and more.

It was a very emotional time that many people are still confused by. Each time a new eccentric voice was added to the growing list of prophetic voices, excuses were made for his methods. Some of the voices came from backgrounds of great brokenness, yet they experienced great grace from the Christian community (grace that would not be given today). Prophets were labeled as abnormal or sovereign, but they were also allowed to be weird, violate relationship, and not be accountable to social standards. Things have changed so much since then, because we have infused the Christian culture with life skills, emotional intelligence, psychology, self-help, true biblical studies, and theology. In other words, we have a move of self-empowerment that creates healthy identity and checks prophetic people at the door for their understanding of emotional and relational health before giving them a platform. We get to go way past the weaknesses and excesses of prophets now, because these days we are seeing a generation of prophetic Christians ready to hear the voice of God and share him in powerful ways.

Paul wrote to the Corinthians about a very key prophetic principle: "The spirits of the prophets are subject to the prophets" (1 Corinthians 14:32 NASB). We use this verse a lot when we expect prophets to be orderly and honoring to the spiritual atmosphere in the room, but this verse actually goes much further than that: It speaks of self-managing, being self-aware, and being accountable to the crowd or community the prophet is prophesying to. There is too little spoken on the governing of the prophetic, but that is because the whole Bible gives a relational framework to the gifts— one that prophecy is supposed to adhere to as its core value system.

Paul and the New Testament writers had no desire to separate ministerial roles from the full accountability of the core message of relationship. There was never a single role in the New Testament— such as missionary, prophet, or pastor—that was talked about more than two or three times. Our main identities, however, as sons and co-inheritors with Jesus, are found as a central thread throughout the New Testament. It's essential to focus on the majors instead of the minors. When we make our identities the central theme of prophetic ministry or the pursuit of the prophetic, it gives prophecy the same importance as every other gift of God's. It's so important that we keep prophetic ministers, and people who prophesy, accountable for their relational skills, not just their prophetic words.

I BLOCKED MY OWN ABILITY TO PROPHESY

In the mid-nineties, I went to a small group filled with really amazing young people I was connected to. I was supposed to speak, and a lot of them were really hoping we could do a prayer time with the goal of hearing God. After I spoke I led them in a prayer, but I felt so blocked! I was asking inside, *What gives?* I was looking for every external reason why nothing felt like it was flowing. I prayed God would change the atmosphere; I prayed we would have faith (meaning that *they* would have faith); I prayed against the enemy.

I just kept praying things and nothing was working. Then I asked God internally again, *Why is this so hard? It feels like there's unbelief in the room.* Then I heard God, who was waiting for me to ask all along, say, *Do you remember when you prayed for that girl over there, Jessica, a year ago and you prophesied some things would happen in her life in a certain timeframe? They didn't, and she's disappointed in you and me. You never took responsibility, and what you are feeling is my desire for you to clean that up.*

I was shocked. I was in a culture that usually blamed the person if the prophecy didn't come true. Wasn't it her fault if my prophecy didn't come true? Wasn't she responsible to steward her word and figure it out? I think most people are like this, looking externally for blocks when sometimes we have created the biggest walls ourselves.

I had really bad self-awareness at the time (and still do at times, but am building it intentionally), so God had to tell me. I didn't feel like it was my responsibility until I put myself in her shoes. I had had a significantly known prophetic minister give me a word a few years before, which would have led me into a greater opportunity with more money and connections . . . and it didn't happen. As a matter of fact, the opposite happened for a while after that. When I went to talk to the minister to ask him if he had insight on why the word hadn't been fulfilled, he was semi-offended and said it was probably because of something in me—that I was disobedient or in sin and had missed it. I was so shocked. I hadn't done anything consciously to deviate from my relationship with God, and I felt like I was advancing, not losing ground. If I had believed what this prophetic minister said to me, I would have put myself in a penalty box or been marginalized in my faith. I would have been devastated if I hadn't worked on having a good solid identity and spiritual maturity.

I knew Jessica must have put a lot of faith in the word I gave her, and she was probably very disappointed. I looked at her and publicly said, "Did the word I gave you a year ago happen at all?"

She looked a little nervous and embarrassed. "No."

"I am so sorry about that. I don't know why some things happen and sometimes I miss it, but I want to take responsibility for that and tell you I am still growing. I hope you can forgive me and know I was just trying to encourage you."

She looked so relieved she got tears in her eyes. "Thank you!" and right then God came in the room. His presence of love came so powerfully I ministered to each person there, including her, and there was no block at all.

ACCOUNTABILITY

I think when people are growing in the prophetic, part of having the spirit of a prophet subject to a prophet is that each person should take responsibility for his ministry as a standard.

Back in the late '90s and early 2000s in Kansas City (as part of Mike Bickle's ministry), I was probably one of the most empowered prophetic voices of the time. One day, after prophesying in a very celebratory public crowd, I was sitting in the hospitality room with Mike and my team. The team was super excited, but Mike, my pastor, challenged me in a very kind way.

"How do you know that the prophecies you give with dates or details for the future happen each time?"

One of the other team members defended me as if it was an attack, despite it being a very great growth question. "Shawn has incredible accuracy; you heard the reports from tonight! We hear feedback all the time! Everyone is always telling you about it!"

Mike was one of my biggest encouragers, and I wasn't insecure about his question because I knew he appreciated me. I was even on that trip because he was the one who had launched my traveling ministry.

He looked at me and said, "One of the mistakes we have made as a ministry culture, that I don't want you to repeat, is that we never looked for the words we gave that weren't right. I bet that 90 percent of the time, if your prophecy doesn't come true over someone's life, he will think God is mad at him or the devil is warring against him, or worse yet, that he blocked something good from coming into his life because of sin. You could alleviate that pressure if you tracked your words for a while to see how many happen the way you prophesy them. I know you get it right most of the time, but I am concerned for the times you don't. If you went back and took responsibility, they would understand that if you were wrong it's not their fault, or God's, or even Satan's. They won't be mad at you for trying, but they might be disappointed."

To my knowledge, Mike had never asked anyone to track before. We did have some team members tracking some of our bigger words at the time, or at least archiving them, but this was at a completely different level. I had never thought of what he was saying. Most people who start to prophesy don't track anything unless they get called out as a ministry and have to prove something. I wanted to be responsible, so I started to track words. We used tape recorders in those days, and I was the only one who had two at times—one for them and one for me. I am so bad at homework that I probably let many slip, but I tried my best to be responsible, especially when it was a really risky or clear word of prophecy for the future.

For about five years I was very particular and tracked everything that was trackable. If there was any word I gave for the future, I would get people's e-mails or phone numbers, even after public meetings, and would e-mail them a day or week after and ask how it went. About sixty percent of the time it was amazing and brilliant, and I grew in faith from those stories. They gave me a lot of courage to keep going. Another 30 percent of the time, people still felt encouraged but couldn't necessarily weigh my word as being accurate, clear, or already fulfilled. Then about ten percent of the time there was no fulfillment.

Out of that ten percent, there were some people who had turned away from God before the word could come true. There were also some terrible warfare type of situations that may have delayed the word. But just as Mike had feared, there were also very innocent people who needed me to take responsibility because they thought they had done something to offend God, even though they were living very connected lives to him. It wasn't their fault. And you know what? It was so easy to take responsibility, and it felt right to do it, even though it didn't (and doesn't) always feel good to have to correct something.

Over those five years I learned how to grow in my gift, authority, and relatability. When you track your words, it gives you an opportunity to learn from your strengths *and* your weaknesses. It causes you to have to be vulnerable as you grow through a deeper level of both insecurity and rejection. You're taking on a level of responsibility that is not always easy, but it is a necessary part of maturing.

I remember going back to Mike Bickle with a sort of report about the process, although he didn't ask for one out of his graciousness. He just wanted me to grow. He was amazed at what I was learning and felt like he probably should have asked a lot more people to take on this kind of responsibility. We tried to install it in our prophetic community for a season, but there was a ton of resistance, mostly from people who had been prophesying for ten or more years and felt entitled to not have to take any responsibility. "It is the people I prophesied to's responsibility to track those words!" But the Bible doesn't say the spirit of a prophet is subject to the body or church he belongs to. It says the spirit of the prophet is subject to the prophet, which means as we take personal responsibility for our words, we begin to grow in personal authority. We disciple our character by tracking, communicating, cleaning up, and celebrating.

TRACKING WORDS IS PART OF OUR RESPONSIBILITY

Obviously there were imbalances in the prophetic, even in the early church days. Paul had to encourage the Thessalonians to not treat prophecy with contempt. I wonder what caused him to have to re-inspire them to honor prophetic ministry. I believe they probably had several experiences, just like every generation has, when some well-known minister pronounced prophetic timetables on things like the rapture, Armageddon, the return of Jesus, or the damnation of a city. The Thessalonians were probably jaded, and some of the bad words probably affected their influence as Christians amongst unbelievers.

There will always be imbalanced personalities in the church. We are not responsible for someone else's theology. We are, however, responsible to set a standard of integrity and accountability amongst our own families and churches. When bright lights shine, darkness looks like darkness and other lights look dull. We don't have to worry about other lights or even darkness; we just have to focus on being as bright as we can and remembering our responsibility to love.

As I have tracked words by asking people later on if things have happened, I have had tons of time to develop emotional intelligence that I wouldn't have developed if I had always maintained a lofty distance. Human immaturity can cause so many misunderstandings, and part of maturing is relating well. It's time we relate and stay open to our mistakes, even if they are not immoral or true failure. Risk and faith are the same thing sometimes, and it should never be embarrassing or have punishing consequences when we are wrong. We may, however, have to have different boundaries in place to grow.

YOU ARE GOING TO DIE IF YOU STAY IN THIS CITY!

I had a pastor from the east coast of America call me and tell me that one of the region's most famous and loved prophets had just prophesied over him, in front of his leadership team, that he would die if he stayed in the city he lived in. Physically die. Like fall down dead and die within two years. The pastor was skeptical, but still nervous. The team was super nervous, because they hadn't heard a word like this before. This prophetic man was very accurate on personal words of other kinds and had a good track record, so they weren't sure if they had to help this pastor (whom they adored) move.

The pastor knew he was called to that city and knew he was supposed to stay, but he was experiencing some friction over his mission in his church. This friction was largely unprocessed, but it could be felt by both the team and his family. He had called me to ask if there was anything he should do. I honestly laughed, even though I didn't mean to. It was just such wrong theology that led to this word.

"Was there a spiritual reason behind the warning?"

"Not specifically," he told me. He shared how he had felt limited by the team and their mentality at times. He lived in New England, where the church was based, but had a west coast background. At times he felt a tension between the cultures, but he always was able to power through that with the passion and love he had for his mission and community.

I asked if anyone on the team had processed with this prophet about this underlying tension. He found out one of the team had talked with the prophet for wisdom and counsel, but he trusted the health of that conversation. I knew that although the team member might have had great health, the prophetic voice might have taken on some limited understanding, which might have swayed his perspective.

"I think this is a distraction. You should tell the prophet that you don't feel that the word is helpful or accurate and that you are going to stay. See if he can handle the rejection of his word or if he holds onto judgment toward you for taking personal authority."

He told me that the prophet was pretty adamant and didn't feel like he could be reasoned with, even though he was such a good man. I explained that to keep a balanced relationship with the prophet long term, he and his team would have to talk to him about this attitude of control with the words he gave. I felt that the prophet might have a more open ear to discuss it after the timeframe was up, at which point they should talk and ask him not to prophesy about death or positional moves with that kind of absolute conviction in the future.

So time went by and the pastor didn't die. He ran a few marathons. He is one of the healthiest men in their late fifties I know, and the church is thriving. The team decided to take me up on my advice and talk to the prophetic voice in a non-confrontational but direct way about several words that hadn't happened—words that involved death, sickness, and money. They identified that when he went after these things, his accuracy was off. Because of his own brokenness in these areas, he didn't have authority in their community, or possibly in his life, to hear God about these things.

When they talked to him about it, he was very open and very sad. He identified that the things he was most concerned about in his own life had been overpowering his prophetic perspective and creating confusion in his ministry, especially when the team processed their own team dynamics and fear with him. He had a fear of death, his finances and financial management skills were always lacking, and he was always sick because of his workaholic schedule. The words he gave that reflected the areas he had more balance in had a healthier connection to God's heart.

He apologized, retracted the words, and agreed to get some counseling so he could get healthy, and I was impressed by that.

CALLED ON THE PHONE BY A PROPHET

"The end purpose of all true prophetic revelation is to build up, to admonish, and to encourage the people of God. Anything that is not directed to this end is not true prophecy." JAMES W. GOLL

A prophet I had heard of in a particular denomination got my phone number and cold called me. He had both a negative and positive reputation for his prophetic ministry. We had never talked, although I knew who he was, but he expected me to know and completely receive him because he was a prophet in his church. He began by telling me about his prophetic authority and that he had a word for me. He didn't ask me if I wanted that word. It was a very one-sided conversation.

He started with the usual prophetic style that was known to his denomination:

"My son, I am pleased with thee. . ."

I am a conversationalist, so this kind of talk always scares me a little, but I know that there are many prophetic styles and I can't get hung up on them. I knew, however, that this word was not healthy. His word was basically that God was going to heal the deep issues of rejection from my father. Then he started on another really hard subject that was very "off," and I interrupted him carefully.

"You know, I so appreciate you taking the time to call. You are speaking about a relationship that is very dear to me, and I don't believe you understand my relationship with my dad. I want to help correct your perception, because I love my dad and honor him a lot. My dad is amazing, and I want to give you some feedback before we move on, because I don't want you thinking he rejected me. He was actually a wonderful dad, and I had no abuse or brokenness in our relationship."

"Well, God showed me you did!" he proclaimed, as if his revelation was greater than my personal truth and experience. I felt like a delusional man was on the other end of the line.

I turned it into a question for him: "Did you have brokenness in *your* relationship with *your* father?"

He said yes.

"Well maybe you are seeing something from your own experience and projecting it on me, or maybe this word is for yourself. Maybe you see yourself in me as a young man, a man who loves the prophetic, and you are trying to guard me from something that happened to you. All of the prophetic message you have given to me doesn't sound like it's for where I am at or where I have been, but it may be for you or from your experience." I was being honest and giving him honest feedback, because I would value that in return.

Love in a way that you would want others to love you.

There was a pause on the phone and then I heard him crying. "I haven't had anyone be this honest with me in years. Thanks for challenging me. You are right. I am going through some rejection and father issues, and I probably projected them on you because I genuinely want your life to be better than what I have had to walk through. I have been so worried about you!"

I was confused because I had never met him, talked to him, or even known him, so why was he worried about me? This kind of concern had turned into a very imbalanced prophetic perspective. Worry for those you have no relationship with produces fear, and fear produces all kinds of warped perspectives.

We were able to talk about him and his life, and he no longer tried to prophesy over me. We had an amazing half-hour conversation after that, but we started it from a great place of honesty and feedback.

CHAPTER 12

RESPONSIBILITY IN REVELATION

YOU ARE THE MOST POWERFUL HUMAN IN YOUR OWN LIFE

I had a woman come up to me at my church and tell me, "You need to go correct that man over there. He prayed for me and told me things that I am uncomfortable with!"

"What did he say?" I asked. She seemed so upset, I thought it must have been terrible.

"He told me God was going to move me and that I was going to start a new business!" She was devastated. She loved her business and her house, and she didn't want to move. She felt like God had placed her there. She was so confused by the stranger's words.

"If you are so convinced he's wrong, why are you so traumatized? He's a complete stranger who is practicing hearing from God for you in a public environment. You are way more powerful than that guy in your life. You know what God is saying to you, and you are guiding your life along the path you think God wants it on. Why didn't you just tell him: 'Thanks for trying to pray for me, but I don't think I am moving or getting a new business. I appreciate you trying to hear from God though.'"

She said she had never thought of the fact that it might be her responsibility to stand up for herself in love and out of kindness for the person praying for her. She wanted to take him to leadership because he had offended her, but the offense came from her own lack of identity or empowerment.

When we receive prophetic words, we have to create an environment of feedback and realistic evaluation. If someone prays over you, you have every right to say you don't agree. You never need to say it in a mean or conflict-laden way; you get to say it through encouragement. It's important that you help coach the environment you are growing in. You are not rejecting a person if you reject his words. You get to receive the person with kindness and compassion and treat him as a human being. If someone gets offended and feels rejected just because you rejected his words, then stay away from him, because he has unhealthy heart boundaries that cause him to use prophecy to control or manipulate the people around him.

Remember my earlier example of Paul and Agabus? Agabus gave Paul an amazing word about not going to Rome because if he did, he would be imprisoned by the Jews and handed over to the Gentiles. Paul told Agabus he had to go because he knew it was God's will. There was no rebuke or falling out over it. It showed that these two mature leaders understood Paul's authority to receive whatever was true from the word given.

The prophetic gift was never given with the understanding that the receiver would suddenly have power over others, or special authority, because of inside information. Prophecy is a demonstration of relational power, not political power. If you won't allow someone to evaluate what you are saying or give you feedback when you prophesy to him, then you are essentially saying you are more important and have more authority, wisdom, and connection to what you are prophesying about than he does. That is the exact opposite goal of prophecy. Prophecy is supposed to connect people to the world around them and the God who loves them, not place you in the center of the equation. Every successful business has a feedback and evaluation model. You evaluate the outcome of any venture by looking for what worked and what didn't to ensure long-term health and growth. Why do we look to a few leaders or pastors to do what we should be doing? We have the authority and the relational responsibility to do it.

I have had hundreds of people prophesy over me because I am a teacher, and that causes people to practice with me. Out of hundreds, only dozens have hit the dead center of the bull's eye. Many more would be frustrating if I had to walk away believing them.

For over fifteen years, one of the main areas people prophesied over me about was my future wife. I didn't get married until I was thirty-seven, so many people who saw me minister just wanted me to have the happiness of marriage. I received so many words about marriage that if I had entertained them all, I would have gone insane. Most of the people who prophesied let their hopes of happiness for me overtake their ability to actually hear a true word from God. Some people had been interceding for me, but again, they took that burden too far by prophesying their hopes for me into being. A few actually had words, although almost none of them were helpful because I was trying to stay focused, and the words given weren't instructional or very encouraging.

According to the words from the masses, my wife was going to be both tall and short; overweight and athletic; have red, brown, and blond hair; and be Asian, African American, and African. She was going to sing, be a worship leader, be a famous actress, be homeless, be an addict, and be a prostitute.

Yes, people really did prophesy all these things, and yes, I still love the prophetic. Because you know what? I know God and I am learning how to discern when it's God talking versus when it's people's desires for me talking. How do we know the difference? It's kind of like bank tellers who learn about counterfeit dollars by counting thousands of real bills. When a counterfeit comes through, they can see the obvious differences because they are so used to handling the real thing. That's how those false words felt for me. I didn't judge the people giving them, because most words came from their desire to encourage me (while others wanted to have authority or connection in my life). I just repositioned their faith in my mind.

Remember when Peter spoke prophetically to Jesus after Jesus said, "I won't be with you in a little while," implying his own death? Peter spoke, convinced he was absolutely right and being prophetic, "This will not happen!!!!" But Jesus said, "Peter, come on now. I know what will happen. Don't come into agreement with human spiritual sentimentality. Zip it, because you sound like the enemy right now, not the Father!"

You need to be real with the people you love. If they are praying something that you don't appreciate, set them straight so they're on the right track in their prayer for you. If someone doesn't know you and prophesies something, shake it off! He isn't your ultimate authority; he is just a believer who is trying to get closer to God's heart and voice! He might even be unhealthy, but who cares? He can't transfer his unhealthy heart culture upon you unless you receive it.

I consider it a great success when people take a risk with a word, so we get an A+ when we try and prophesy. The grade is already set, even if you don't get the information or the prophetic word correct. The problem that can happen in your prophetic journey is when you don't take responsibility for your mistakes (the words you got wrong). Stubbornness takes your grade down to a D or F. When you aren't willing to grow and educate yourself along the way, you aren't impacting or helping those around you.

LEARNING FROM EXPERIENCE AND BEING ACCOUNTABLE TO KNOWLEDGE

What happens when a woman prophesies marriage over each of her unmarried friends and none of them get married? She can learn by going back and taking responsibility for each word, and accept that her zeal was greater than her authority. She can keep her words for prayer instead of declaration. How about a man who prophesies great financial breakthrough to all of his buddies, but notices that only some progress rapidly while others don't get any financial relief or change. He can learn the difference between his enthusiasm and hopeful desire for his friends versus the timing and voice of God.

We learn from what we are consistently wrong and right in. While pastoring prophetic people, I have found that there are some subjects they are more prophetically accurate in—usually areas they have more authority to speak into. I have one friend who is brilliant with words about business and direction but terrible with words about marriage and family. It doesn't mean he can't give words on marriage and family, but he should be way softer in how he shares them because of his record of low accuracy and limited intuitiveness in that area. Put him in front of a business group, though, and he is usually right on the mark. We can learn which area we are gifted and more accurate in—our area of grace—by being faithful to take risks as they come up in our hearts.

WEIGHING OUR PROPHETIC EXPERIENCE

1 Corinthians 14:29 talks about the fact that all prophecy should be weighed. What is this "weighing"? One thing I have realized is that we misinterpret a lot of things as "a word from God" when they are actually emotional responses to circumstances or hormones:

God told me I will marry you!

Sometimes they come from desperation:

God told me I WILL get this job!

Then the job doesn't come, but we wanted it so badly that we claimed it by a desperation-based faith. Sometimes it's something we are hoping for:

We will win the lottery!

We have to weigh our personal and corporate prophetic experiences so we can grow. This is often misunderstood, because then people feel obliged to create a tracking structure that becomes just one more responsibility that never gets done. Let me give you some great examples of how you can weigh a prophecy you are giving (or that is given to you):

1. Get feedback: Give the prophetic person (who has prophesied to you) feedback. Tell him what connected and what has yet to connect (or may never connect) in your heart or spirit. As a person gets feedback, it starts to grow him. He can begin to feel when a word is 100 percent accurate and/or when it isn't. He can sense which parts felt inspired by the Holy Spirit and actually connected with his audience versus which parts felt like human encouragement or his hopes for good things to happen. He can also then start to learn what is disconnected, uninspired, and doesn't land at all.

I had a friend who was trying to meet his birth parents, and he had a lot of father wounds. His whole filter during that time was one of fathers wounding their children and abandoning them. He would give words that were sometimes given through this filter, along with some very real encouragements. After about ten times of feedback, he was able to see that all of the father wounds he was going after in others weren't registering and had nothing to do with them and everything to do with his own process. He knew to back off of these sentiments while in prayer ministry times with others and to focus more on the other stuff, which seemed accurate and helpful each time.

The more we are self-aware, the more often we will remove ourselves from our ministry time when necessary. The more we can know what is effective, the more we will focus on being effective. When we hear critical feedback, it is not necessarily negative feedback because it will cause us to grow.

We can have a critical analysis without a critical spirit.

On the flip side, when you get the feedback that you are right or you carried authority, you become more sensitive to doing it again or having that same impact in the future. You learn prophetic authority by seeing where it manifested in the past.

2. As a person trying to grow in prophecy, track all information that is weighable and get feedback on it. If you can track what you are saying, write it down and write down the contact info. Weigh it by watching it happen or not happen.

I have prophesied to many individuals, businesses, and churches that God is going to give them a building in which they can follow their hearts' desires. Not all of the buildings would be free, but the Holy Spirit would guide them to amazing deals or upgrades, or place them into buildings perfectly designed for them. So far I have prophesied fifty-three correctly, and then three haven't happened in the timeframe I gave. I now try not to give the timeframes because they don't matter, unless it's really clear (like a few of the fifty-three I got right). Some of them were just intuitive feelings about the timeframe with a definite, clear word about the building itself. I am learning when to take the risk and give a timeframe with the prophetic word, and when not to.

Feedback and evaluation are never supposed to be a tearing-down time; they are supposed to be natural and helpful growth tools. If you are insecure or lack identity in an area, you might feel overwhelmed by this part of the responsibility. There is no reason to start dogging yourself about why things didn't happen. The bigger cause for celebration is that you tried! You went in with the goal of loving on someone through practicing spiritual gifts! You get an A+, but you still have to be open to learn. My mentor used to say, "If my prophecy is right, then bless you! If it is wrong, then bless me for trying. Either way both, or one of us, are blessed." She always said this to help people overcome rejection and fear when trying to prophesy.

3.   When you *give* words, record them and listen to them again later to weigh their different parts. When you *receive* a word, individually or as a community, listen to it again in different seasons of time, and see if you feel differently about it in the future. Sometimes time and space can make us feel differently about things (like your lingering love for a narcissistic ex).

I remember when an Asian billionaire gave me a word about becoming a billionaire, by starting an Asian-based business, while still in my thirties. He said he saw me as a young version of himself. Initially I felt very excited and empowered by the word, although I was confused because I didn't want to start a business at the time, especially in Asia. His words felt very alive in my emotional being because I am an adventurer by nature, and the whole time I was with him, I dreamed of how it could happen. He introduced me to opulence in the few days I got to hang out with him, and it was all very exciting. I dreamed of the lifestyle of the rich for a minute and thought about how my future riches could affect social justice. It was a fun dream to dream. Then I came home, a year went by, and

I had no feeling of inspiration from the word for me at all. I knew after another year that this man had a great heart, but he had not heard from God for me. There was no confirmation, and it didn't motivate me at all to start any sort of business, let alone in Asia.

I didn't become a billionaire in Asia in my thirties.

4. Get feedback as quickly as possible while the word is fresh. Or if you are receiving the word, give the people who prophesied immediate feedback. Immediate doesn't mean right after, but make sure to share with them what really mattered in the word. If there is something like a word of knowledge that was off, share it with them as well in a positive, constructive way. The more we share what is working with those who are trying, the faster they will grow. The prophetic is a skillset based on relationship, so it will only grow by relational feedback.

Practically, I try and give the majority of people who pray prophetically for me feedback and encouragement (*when they are someone I have a connection to—friends I can text or write to through social media or e-mail*). I have found they really appreciate my taking the extra time to connect, thanking them for their effort, and sharing what was special. Here is an example of one I wrote recently:

The word was from a social media friend:

Shawn, I really feel like your church is about to go through a season of evangelistic focus and you are going to see salvations. I also feel like God wants to bring so much salvation that I saw fifteen church locations in the city of Los Angeles! I feel like you are going to birth all kinds of locations! At our church we have three campuses, and I feel like it will be something like that. I also heard God say, "Well done for loving people in the entertainment industry." Lastly, does your best friend have blond hair, because I felt like God was going to use a blond man in his fifties who might be named Dwayne. Lastly, I heard the song "Catch a falling star" from Perry Como.

Here was my response and feedback:

Thanks so much! Our church is focusing on evangelism a lot this year, and we have already had quite a few new converts and are excited about seeing people saved. If you had said that at any other time, it may not have been true, but this year we are going after it more deliberately than we ever have!

We have started home groups all around the city, and I believe there are around fifteen. We have no intention of starting campuses the way your church has at this time, but we did just start these groups and that's encouraging—probably similar to what you are seeing—and that really encourages me. Thanks for acknowledging our heart for the entertainment industry, it's one of the things you know we are passionate about. Also, I don't have a friend named Dwayne and my best friend is a Guatemalan with black hair. I'll shelve that one. Lastly, the song almost brings tears to my eyes because it's super significant. God told us through a little girl in Africa, and a little girl here in America, that we would be catching falling celebrities and loving on them, not letting them get away from their eternal destiny. This has been happening as well. A nine-year-old girl in America sang the song to me. She had no idea we worked in the entertainment industry and her mom had no idea where she had heard or learned the song.

Thanks so much!

Shawn Bolz

In my feedback, the person could hear the wide variety of where she was spot on, what she said out of connection to what she was related to, what she already knew about me and was encouraging (out of that knowledge), and what didn't work. Lastly, she got to my heart by just mentioning a simple song that meant so much to me. You can learn so much with just one feedback.

5. When you give a corporate word, let it be weighed. Don't try and fit any details in to make it work more. For the leadership receiving a corporate word: Weigh the word based on everything else God is saying to your leadership and community.

I have seen people go way off their current priorities and goals after getting an exciting word from someone not connected to their community or connected to them relationally. Any words you get from people like this should be confirming, or at least feel like they flow with the things you are currently building with God. If a word doesn't fit, you should shelve it and wait for confirmation. People who are not relationally involved with you don't know your story, your journey, what God is saying or has said, what your community around you is carrying, etc. So when they prophesy over you, they may say big exciting things that have no relevancy at all . . . but the words *feel* exciting, or you let them steal attention away from what you really need to focus on. Lots of times it's easy for the visiting prophet to unintentionally exaggerate the word because of the lack of relationship. I have seen a prophet come into a city and prophesy over a mom-and-pop business that it was going to be one of the most influential businesses in the city, when what God was really trying to convey was that he was going to use the couple to influence others in the city through their business.

Another example is when I have seen people prophesy over pastors, "You are the one God's chosen to bring such and such to the earth!" when they are just called to be some of the many faithful who carry that calling. In other words, part of a group's responsibility to weigh a word is to sift out exaggeration and potential elitism and discern which sphere of authority and influence the word is really for. If God is saying to the business leader, "I want to give you more influence" (and that is a directive to help him get involved with the next city job fair, the chamber of commerce, the mayor's brunch, etc.), but the prophetic person is prophesying that the leader have the wealthiest, most influential company in the country, the leader may miss his time to really benefit from the theme of the word.

One popular, influential prophetic minister was invited to a church in Texas that he has a lot of chemistry with. This church is very isolated and doesn't spend any time developing relationships with city leaders or other churches, so it is encouraging a cultish behavior with some elitism. This minister was unaware of its negative impact on the local culture. Because he is celebrated there, he began to prophesy that they were the "APOSTLES OF THE CITY." (Picture a Mexican ad voiceover.)

The problem with this word was they were doing no apostolic work in their city. They used the word to inflate their sense of importance by giving themselves the title of apostles—over their own work of around one hundred people. The city still viewed the church leaders as strange, useless, and self-involved, but this word empowered so much self-entitlement that the pastors were demanding that other churches treat them with an added level of respect because they had received such a prophecy. They would show up to city church gatherings and want special seating and parking, when they hadn't contributed in any tangible way to the church in their city. That shows you how bad it can get when church culture can misuse prophecy and use it as a self-serving endorsement of bad behavior—which usually happens when a church is not connected to reality and relationship, both with God and people.

PROPHETIC RESPONSIBILITY

Please practice accountability by tracking your words and encouraging regular feedback. No one will ever want your growth as much as you do. I used to have a team around me who did a lot of this work for me, but it just didn't bring in the same fruit as when I did it myself. I still try to track certain prophecies and get feedback on them. It's true that doing so does slow you down. You will have to stop and get people's contact information, and you will have to have more conversations than you intended. The prophetic is a very social gift set. For every word you track, you'll have to create one to two more conversations around it. The days of an isolated prophetic personality are over.

Honest human moment: Sometimes I don't want to give as many words because I know they will create future conversations, but what amazing conversations they are!

Another way to define prophetic responsibility is to call it relational responsibility, an essential skillset for anyone who wants to grow in authority. You can't have relational responsibility unless you have some level of self-awareness or emotional intelligence. We are constantly trying to get those skillsets plugged into our people. We have seen that most people who act weirdly wouldn't if they knew not to.

THE PROPHET GEORGE (NAME CHANGED)

We were hosting a regional prophetic class once, and a lot of us came to set up early and organize. Some of the new students came to help as well, and one of them came up to me. He looked normal enough, except for his eyes and facial expression. His face was speaking for him: *I am waiting to be called on in class to speak.* He was desperate to tell me something. He was very old in his style and genre of prophetic ministry, and he hadn't aged or grown well in his gift.

"I am Prophet George Band, and I have many messages from God for you! God has sent me here to instruct many!" He was so excited to meet me, but it didn't feel like helpful excitement, especially because we were leading the prophetic class and had never heard of him. We were immediately a little leery of how he was inviting himself in as a teacher to our class rather than as a student, a friend, or a leader.

"Hi, Prophet George!" I said, shaking his hand. "Let's get to know one other. Can I ask you some questions?"

"Of course!" he said, waiting for some great spiritual question to come from me.

"Where did you go to celebrate Christmas last year?"

He was so confused. He looked at me as if I couldn't have really asked "the prophet" such a menial question. I think he chose to answer it just because it confused him so much.

"Um, I don't remember." He looked at me, his eyes wondering if this was a serious question. When he could tell it was, he answered, "I went to a pastor friend's house."

"That's awesome. Is this pastor one of your closest friends? Was it here in the city?"

"No, I had just met him and his wife, and it was a few hours away. They pastor a small Pentecostal church that I minister at sometimes."

"How about the last few years before that?"

He couldn't remember. He thought that maybe one Christmas he went to a soup kitchen to help, and he felt really good about that response.

"How about birthdays? Who celebrates your birthday every year with you, and who do you call on their birthdays?" I asked.

He had no one he could think of that was very consistent, and he was confused as to why I was asking him such irrelevant questions, but they were important to me in this introduction.

"Have you been to the hospital for anything in the last few years?" I asked.

"Yes. I had to have a surgery."

"Who came to visit you while you were there? Or did anyone go with you?"

"Well, some women from a church came and prayed for me." He hesitated.

"That must have been a very hard time," I said, with genuine compassion. "I get to pastor this church with some of my best friends. Who are your best friends?"

He had none.

"Prophet George, I really, really value the connectedness of relationship to our prophetic gifting, and you are so relationally disconnected that I am not sure I want to receive spiritually from you. You are welcome in this class to grow and gain wisdom about people and how prophecy works in the context of relationship, but I don't trust the way you do your ministry because it's not grounded in friendship. I understand if that feels limiting to you. Does that make sense?"

"Well, yeah. No one has ever told me that before, *but I am a prophet!*" He sounded somewhat sad and also defensive. It was all he had valued, fought for, and owned.

"That's wonderful that you are a prophet, but I don't need someone with a tool in his tool belt; I need people here who want to fight for relationship and use that tool to build the kingdom of love. If you can do that, please stay." I walked away to start the class.

I could tell he wasn't sure if he wanted to stay or go. He was used to going places where he could stand up and share a word people clapped to. He was used to prophesying over strangers all over the city, but he had no friends. I don't know if he was even happy about any other part of his life, because he had nothing he valued outside of his prophetic gift.

He decided to stay in the class, and you know what? He came a long way! He made friends! He celebrated birthdays! His was celebrated as well. He went to movies and potlucks, and he invited people to the first apartment he had ever lived in (before this he lived in group homes and ministry homes that had no personal space). He permanently slipped out of his performance mode because he was in family.

TO HAVE PROPHETIC RESPONSIBILITY IS TO KNOW WHOM YOU GET TO LOVE

You want to grow in authority to speak powerful words? Grow in love! Pray and fall in love with your spouse, your family, your friends, your coworkers, your church, your neighbors, and your city and you will have spiritual perspectives to share that will have ears that want to listen everywhere. Some people think that prophetic influence is hard to measure because they think you have to count up how many words you have impacted people with. That is not a measure of prophetic influence. The real measure is to self-evaluate how well you carry people with spiritual love in your heart, so that every time you speak to them, you call them into fullness. This influence is easily felt and measurable.

CHAPTER 13

PUTTING IT INTO PRACTICE

Remember this: You get to prophesy if you want to! You get to see more fruit than any other generation has ever seen! It is your time!

The prophetic gifts in most circles are expected to just happen. There is still no training room, no practice area, no growth scale. We have to burst this bubble and release an environment in which people can grow.

My first mentor in the prophetic is still one of my most favorite people. She helped me to have faith that I could hear from God, and she made everything I attempted in the prophetic feel validated by sharing her own experience and faith. We would pray for people together and I would share the baby-est of visions and she would add to it and make it a homerun. She would give me feedback that was super honest and sometimes corrective, but she always believed in me. It helped set me up to want to grow, not just in hearing God but in helping others.

IT TAKES A LOT OF PRACTICE

The biggest thing she planted in my heart was the awareness that it was going to take a lot of practice before I felt comfortable with myself and my gifts. She would turn everything into practice, but in a fun way. Going to the movies? Let's go pray for the ticket takers. Going to the grocery store? Let's pray for the homeless guy. Going to have fun in the park? Let's pray for the people playing baseball. She was fearless in her approach to growth, and it made me value stepping out over and over.

For some reason, many people think prophets should be able to bypass the practice and skill-building process. Can you imagine listening to Joel Osteen's first fifty messages? I am sure one or two would have been very inspirational to those who knew him, but most of us would have thought, *This guy has a lot of growth to do. I am going to listen to Jack Hayford instead.* No one would have paid for me to come speak based on my first five years of ministry, but Mike Bickle and the Kansas City prophetic team let me tag along and speak during main sessions anyway. It was their grace, not the host churches, that made a way for me.

In other words, it takes hundreds if not thousands of attempts at public speaking and teaching before you become decent and re-latable, and that is if you are doing it in an educated way. For some reason we expect people to prophesy as experts in their first sea-sons of trial, but it just never happens that way in a context that can be maintained.

When I lived in Kansas City, we would deliberately share rides with lots of people from our local church and practice the prophetic in the car. One way we would practice is by praying for friends and family that we knew but the others in the car didn't. They would try to hear God about our relatives and then ask questions to see if they heard right. "Is it a woman in her thirties? Is it an older man? Are they starting new jobs?" It sounded like twenty questions at first, because we were all just trying to hear God together and were practicing in a safe place. We would all get a ton of things wrong. Even I, leading these times, got so many pieces of information wrong . . . but then something shifted. God honored our hunger and we started to get great accuracy. We learned in those times to feel the difference between our thoughts and God's. We would feel the different weight on some of our impressions versus others that we were emotionally attached to.

Doing things like this for twenty years has helped me have faith for this current influx of words of knowledge. Giving words of knowledge is so risky, because one is either true or it isn't. There is no room for interpretation. All these years of practice, growing in faith and understanding, growing in my relationship with God, and learning my unique ways of hearing him have helped immeasurably. These days I get a lot of word association words, so I will see someone who reminds me of one of my friends growing up, and I will find out this is God's way of showing me he shares the same name or birthdate. Each one of us hears differently.

I was taken out to eat by one man who had basically written off my ministry as a Christian circus show, but was still intrigued. I knew he was very wealthy and influential in the country we were in. We talked for hours over dinner with his wife and my friend/assistant. At one point, before we were to leave, his wife asked us to pray for them. I wanted to pray with intention because we had built great rapport, but I knew he wasn't into prophecy, and I wanted to give God an available chance to go as deep into this man's heart with his love as possible.

I remembered one time on a long road trip when we were trying to guess each other's bank account numbers. I should say we were eager in faith and praying for it, but it was as prophetic as trying to get the lottery numbers. We epically failed that day. As I was remembering our trial and error over those numbers, I started to see a number form in my head. It was very long, and I started to say it out loud because I knew I would forget it. It was a mix of letters, numbers, and symbols. The man gasped when I got to the middle of it. My friend thought I was having a breakdown, because he said I sounded like a computer reading code. After about twenty-something characters, I was done.

"How do you know that number?!" He was angry, his knuckles firmly grasping the table.

"I just heard it from God. He told me he cares about security more than you do."

It took a second, but he said, "God really does speak. That's my most private bank account number, and I change it almost monthly. I can't believe this!"

His wife laughed and said, "Even I don't know it! He won't tell me!"

We were able to minister beautifully over them. Isn't that amazing that all those times of practicing and even failing prepared me to take that risk? Trying all those years ago set a pattern in my heart that allowed God to pick up where I had left off—years before. What felt like an epic fail was what gave me the courage to look again.

REWARDING RISK

In our local church and friendship environment, risk should be rewarded, not just success. It takes so much courage and faithfulness to keep trying to prophesy or give words of knowledge. Picture it as being more of an athletic training. When I was learning how to prophesy, we had an old-fashioned church directory with just names, phone numbers, and sometimes addresses. I made it my goal to call seven to fourteen people a week for almost two years so I could pray for them and try and encourage them. We had thousands of members, so I never got through the whole directory, but I learned every day from my time of prayer ministry with them.

After a few hundred, I had collected some skill in starting the conversation, ending the prayer, connecting what I was seeing to their hearts, etc. It takes time and practice.

CELEBRATING FRUIT

Once you start to track together as a community over someone's individual or corporate words, you get to celebrate his fruit. My close friends have consistently pointed out how much faith I built in them by pursuing huge visions over my life, or by stepping out and prophesying over others. It is so rewarding to be around others long term and share the testimonies of God's goodness. Part of celebrating fruitful words only happens in the context of committed community. Do you hear correctly and in ways that empower the world around you? Your family and friends will keep those celebrations about your prophecies living on.

BUILDING HISTORY WITH A COMMUNITY

"Build history with God and he will build history through you." BILL JOHNSON

As you build a history of accurate and connected prophetic words, the world around you begins to listen to you or look to you. People will begin to look to God in you to bring transformation to their issues and lives. Once you start to build a personal history of what is working and you have a measured, trackable list of your words that came to pass, you will begin to grow in long-term influence. Of course, there will always be new people and groups to meet and connect to that won't know or relate to your history, but building it in one sphere helps you to have boldness in others. Seeing God through your history will cause you to be more confident, take greater risks, and believe for more. Hearing God and seeing the fruition of your words is addicting, because you see that these gifts and your relationship to God make a huge difference in the world around you.

David killed a lion and a bear, so spiritually he was ready for Goliath. He knew he had walked out a prophetic journey with those animals, so the Philistines were no match for the power of God working in him. I remember when I was brought into one of the business boards I was on and they asked me to pray with them over their decisions. It wasn't so that I could hear God about each one of them, but because I could help them discern what they were feeling and hearing. I sometimes got revelation too. After a few years of successful risk taking, giving prophetic words, and discerning what God was saying to them, they brought me in on a big decision.

They asked me to pray with them about the acquisition of a certain hotel. They were not in the hotel business, but this really great deal and business had come up. We prayed together for a bit and I got a "picture" of the hotel, the current problems with it, the market in that region going up after three years, and even the décor. After praying, they had enough courage, based on my history with them and what they were feeling themselves (about the business and from God) to take the risk and buy the hotel. It was a great investment that made them hundreds of thousands of dollars in ten months which, for their small financial business, was an amazing benefit.

When we take the time to build history, pray together, and try and hear together, we create a trusted relationship of faith and inspiration that few other areas in our life can keep up with.

TRANSLATING GOD

In trying to hear God, we also have to interpret him, much like a foreign language interpreter for the UN. We are trying to translate God.

Immigrants who pre-learn English in their native countries find out that their knowledge of the vocabulary and grammar rules isn't always helpful in the US. When they speak the English they learned, their native voice inflections can cause our familiar words to mean different things. To become successful interpreters/translators/English speakers, they also have to learn the local slang and cultural nuances. They have to understand the human culture around them, not just the words. We are also called to translate God's words—sent from his kingdom culture, relational nuances, and spiritual language—to the people who need to really understand who he is.

This takes a process of really understanding how God talks and relates things to you. When you read Paul's writings, you can hear in the language he used that sports were important to him. He talked about being an athlete and going after life like we are going to win the race. God used this language to transcend direct principles so that we would relate to his words more easily. Peter didn't understand how to relate to Gentiles, so God had to use a vision of a sheet of unclean foods he could relate to. The Romans created an altar to an unknown god just so they didn't offend any gods they hadn't acknowledged, and then the apostles were able to use it to preach to them about the kingdom.

You cannot translate what you do not know or understand, and the type of knowing we are talking about is not knowledge based; it's heart based. You are translating the culture of heaven and the heart of the Father. If you want to grow, get to know his heart culture. Look at all the ways he is talking to you. Study history. Find out how he has spoken into church movements around you. Try and see him in current popular culture right now. Practicing this will cause you to see a whole new level of God.

Self-Enforcing Personal Accountability Tip: Do you want my tip that will cause you to grow faster? I gave you the pitch to track, to measure, to weigh. Now it's time to make a commitment to grow in an educated way so you can master the prophetic gifts. There are people who have a knack for prophecy or a sovereign calling to move in it, but unlike music, which takes talent, we were all created to hear from God. We can all develop the skills and the relationship to make it wonderful. Track and you will grow faster.

LISTEN TO OTHER GOD STORIES

One of the most fruitful ways to grow is to treasure hearing others' God stories. It will teach your spirit what is possible and will help you to take new risks that your imagination has never seen. Your spirit is looking for new ways to give away God's love, and it is easy when you fill yourself with authentic and doable stories. I can't tell you how many stories I have fed my faith with. It has helped me to set a high bar for my own journey. I have this feeling that God never puts anything in front of us that we cannot replicate. If we see it, he is imparting faith for a similar occurrence or testimony in our lives. When I hear pastors, public speakers, missionaries, or business people share amazing God stories, I know that listening to them can be an invitation to recreate them.

Do you listen that way? It is your invitation as well!

RECOGNIZE YOUR OWN GROWTH

Don't get hung up on what you do not have or what is not happening. Focus on being grateful for what is there, what you are accomplishing, and what is true revelation, and God will multiply it.

It is time to translate God to this world! You are his voice. Go into every place he can get glory!

ABOUT THE AUTHOR

Shawn Bolz is the author of *The Throne Room Company, Keys to Heaven's Economy: An Angelic Visitation from the Minister of Finance*, and *The Nonreligious Guide to Dating and Being Single*, and he is also an international speaker, pastor, and prophet.

Shawn has been a minister since 1993, and these days he is well-known for his strong prophetic gift and fresh biblical perspective. Shawn taught, ministered, mentored, and prophesied at Metro Christian Fellowship with Mike Bickle in the '90s, and in the early 2000s he joined the International House of Prayer in Kansas City. After leaving Kansas City in 2005, he founded and still pastors Expression58 in Los Angeles—a mission base and church focused on training and equipping Christians, encouraging the creative arts, and loving people in the entertainment industry and the poor.

Shawn is a board member and representative of The Justice Group based in Los Angeles, California, with whom he has worked on social justice issues and missions operations around the world. He and his wife are also the founders of Bolz Ministries—created to inspire and empower God's love around the world, and iCreate Productions—formed to produce exceptional media that motivates and transforms culture.

Shawn currently lives in Los Angeles, California, with his wife Cherie, and their two beautiful daughters.

ACKNOWLEDGMENTS

I now love words of affirmation and love giving credit where credit is due, so I put this in the back of the book so that readers who have an aversion to sappiness don't have to read them. This is pretty much a thank-you to people who were specifically involved in my prophetic process and ministry.

I want to first thank my wife, Cherie, who has taught me and cultivated with me a love that has grounded me and given me healthy boundaries. Your boundaries for love and your protection of relationships you value are such a model of health and life to me. You are an inspirer of inspirers, and although I have to share you with the world, you are mine. Our family is my favorite thing ever, and your belief and celebration in me are so important. I love you and the girls so much.

I want to thank my parents for teaching me that the Holy Spirit didn't shrink to a junior version of himself inside of me. Larry and Stacia, you drew his voice out of us kids from the time we were little. You discipled us and modeled the supernaturally natural life of Christianity, and I am forever grateful. You are my parents and spiritual parents, and my heart needs no upgrades thanks to you guys being my primary mentors. How beautiful!

I want to thank Theresa Lea, my teen and young adult mentor. You always used your prophetic gift to go so deep with God, more so than anyone I have ever met. Your relationship with the Holy Spirit inspired your relationship with the voice of God, and it affected everyone around you. I am so grateful to you.

I want to thank Expression58, my church, for being the incubator of the prophetic love culture we have (in progress) that I talk about in this book. There are too many of you to name, and these pages would be way too full if I started, but you guys model people in the process of empowerment. Your grace for me has allowed me to explore this new season of the prophetic, and given me grace to travel so much. Thanks, Jona and Jennifer Toledo, our co-pastors, for being the friends I need, and for your amazing lives that inspire me all the time. You both teach on how to hear God all around the world, from children to adults, and you have become a role model family for us.

I want to thank Mike Bickle and everyone involved in my prophetic development during my time in Kansas City, specifically David Dreiling, a true Jew, who was the first one to launch me and modeled that you don't have to be bigger than anyone else around to have fun. I know you are in heaven now, and we miss you. And to Jill Austin, whose legacy is one who made the Holy Spirit our friend and told me thousands of hours of God stories while listening to mine. There were never two people who interrupted each other more.

I want to thank Rick Joyner and Morning Star Ministries for being pioneers and for receiving me as an extended family member. Rick, David Yarnes, and the rest of the Morning Star friends and family, I am grateful!

I want to thank Heidi and Rolland Baker for modeling what hearing God's voice can do to transform the poor of the earth. You have personally grounded me in the love that this book speaks of, just by example and the time we have spent together.

I want to thank Che and Sue Ahn and HRock/HIM for being so good for my growth and heart. Thanks for relationship and all the opportunities to grow and give away who I am. I love being part of the family.

Finally, I want to thank Bill and Beni Johnson and the Johnson family, Kris and Kathy Valotton, Danny and Sheri Silk, and the rest of my Bethel family. You give me such great joy to be a part of your family. (There are too many of you to name, so I'm sticking with the moms and dads.) Thank you for being the place of love and faith, and for giving grace for this new prophetic season to emerge. I have full courage because of your full faith, and I am at home in your love.

KEYS TO HEAVEN'S ECONOMY

So begins the unfolding of Shawn Bolz's visitations from God's heavenly messenger, His Minister of Finance.

Heavenly resources have only one purpose—that Jesus Christ would receive His full reward and inheritance in our age. Just as God held nothing back from Solomon, who longed to build a tabernacle for God on earth, God will hold nothing back from a generation of people who long to bring Jesus everything that belongs to Him!

God is about to release finances and resources to reshape the Body of Christ on the earth. God is looking for those who desire an open door experience with the One who is the Master of all keys, Jesus.

http://bolzministries.com/product/keys-to-heavens-economy/

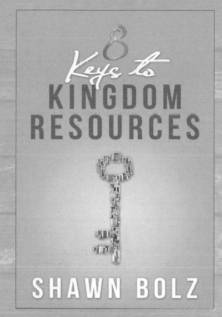